MW01007938

"Stuffed with yearning and wit, heartbreak and triumph, this book is simply storytelling at its peak that calls to mind Anne Lamott, Garrison Keillor, and John Irving: a story that's funny, touching, a pure delight to read, and perfect for any father who is deeply in love with his kids."

– Marc Elmer, father of a child with autism

"This is a fundamentally serious book — how can a human being not question the goodness of God when put face to face, every day, with a suffering child? But despite the seriousness of the topic, Johnny Bollow endows the work with an undercurrent of humor, a deep affection for his son, and a reverence for his wife's extraordinary wisdom and grace that shines through everything, and these elements combine to suffuse the whole with a kind of mysterious joy."

– Lee R. Cerling, Ph.D., University of Southern California

"As a mom of a child with special needs, this book gave the inner thoughts in the recesses of my soul permission to come out and be real, acknowledged, grieved, and pursued by love. Sam's story inspires me to continue to look for the unexpected ways in which my sweet boy is trying to tell me what his world is like. More stories like this need to be told not just for a parent like me, but for the communities around us. Beautifully written."

– Laura Gossman, mother of a child with autism

"Every day we wake to mysteries: mystery of the cosmos, mystery of the human brain, mystery of God, and, for some of us, the mystery of parenting special needs children. In *Remember, You're the Greatest*, Johnny Bollow opens wide the window to his soul. He invites us onto his journey, picking up tools as he comes by them along the way only to find that most are not fit for the job at hand. I cried, I laughed — a lot — and was moved from one chapter to the next with the winds of hope ever present in Johnny's writing. His story is not simply a great book for the special needs community. It is a great book, period."

– Mark Spinelli, father of a son with Down Syndrome

"It is only through the imperfect and the broken that the miraculous is made possible. So writes Johnny Bollow in his beautifully rendered story about three generations of fatherhood. You will laugh. You will cry. You will shake your head in amazement. But most of all, you will walk into the rest of your life inspired to face your particular challenges with grace, integrity, and bravery. As you read these pages, dear reader, just a simple request. Take off your sandals, for you stand on holy ground."

– Timothy J. Patterson, MFT

"Johnny Bollow's narrative reveals the holiness and the humility of parenting, wrapped in lamentation and hope. His words speak of the common core of loving our children — all of them. He shares the profound mystery, the loss, and the renewal."

– James N. Sells, Ph.D.
Endowed Chair
Christian Thought and Mental Health Practices
Regent University

"Readers will delight in the tale of three generations of the Bollow family, enjoying a magical foray into the wonder of boyhood, the entrance into parenthood, and then a catapult into a world full of unexpected pain and heartrending diagnosis. Through it all, Bollow writes with a stark vibrance, each chapter echoing with sounds and sensations, color and texture. The reader is fully immersed, and imprinted with wild hope and a burning desire to love everyone dear to them with a deeper, truer love."

– Susan Reedy, MA, autism specialist

"Yes, it is one man's heartbreaking and soul-touching journey as the father of a special needs child, the toll it takes on the family, and the sorrow of lost dreams. But this book reminds us that we can make a difference when we love another human deeply, when we show up in suffering, and allow imperfection to be beautiful."

– Juli Chaffee, MSW, LCSW

"As a pastor and a parent, my observation is that parents of kids with special needs often feel isolated and forgotten by God. And as your child grows, the chronic grief and exhaustion don't usually wane. Johnny Bollow's book is a breath of fresh air to lonely parents. He is not afraid to ask the difficult questions and be vulnerable about suffering. And the way he weaves stories of his own father with his experience as Sam's father, points to God's deep love and abiding presence through it all. Masterful storytelling, humor, and honesty that lets parents know they are not alone on their journey."

– Rev. Julie Ono, family care pastor
Evergreen Baptist Church, Los Angeles

"The vulnerability that Johnny Bollow is willing to step into wholeheartedly in his new book will be a resource for families of children with special needs and the professionals who work with them. He paints a beautiful and complex picture that captures the importance of celebrating neurodiversity. But, courageously, he speaks not only of the light but of the grittier, darker places that have touched the lives of he and his family. This is a must-read for anyone who loves someone with special needs."

– Jackie Stemen, MS, ACSW, parent coach for autism

"As a physical therapist, I have been privileged to work with hundreds of special needs children. But in pediatrics, we treat the family just as much as the child. Johnny's richly detailed yet honestly unvarnished account of his journey as both a son and a father gives one an unobstructed view of what 'family' is truly like in the home of a child who is special. Equal parts heart-wrenching and laughter inducing, at its core it speaks to the message of God's perfect love — filtered up through an imperfect son, to the greatest earthly father he could ever have. A great book. Go read it."

– Jaime Clevenger, PT, MPT
physical therapist for special needs children

"Most parenting books are about the wins, but very few address what happens when you're not winning. I don't know when I've been so deeply moved. This book is as deep as it gets, and the honesty, pain, and joy in Johnny's story makes it a must-read for every mom and dad."

– Mark Pickerill, co-lead pastor
Christian Assembly, Los Angeles

REMEMBER, YOU'RE THE GREATEST

HOW ONE SPECIAL NEEDS BOY
TAUGHT HIS FATHER ABOUT LOVE, GOD,
AND EVERYTHING ELSE

A MEMOIR

JOHNNY BOLLOW

AND DRAM

To be a witness does not consist
in engaging in propaganda,
nor even in stirring people up,

but in being a living mystery.

It means to live in such a way
that one's life would not make sense
if God did not exist.

EMMANUEL CÉLESTIN SUHARD

CONTENTS

A PRAYER IN THE DARK

I walk into their bedroom. My toddler, Finley, sleeps peacefully, flying to bright planets in his spaceship pajamas. But the landscape of Sam's dreams is broken by thunderbolts. He is seizing.

I kneel down and stroke his three-year-old head as it quivers and jerks. I quietly say that I'm here, that he's going to be okay. But I don't know if I believe that anymore. I twist my fists into his bedspread and bury my face there.

In a whisper wet with tears I plead, "Make it stop. Please, heal him. Why don't You do something?"

I cannot account for what came next, but in my mind I hear a still small voice:

> *Don't you understand? He will be great.*

Sam gets past the worst of the seizure, the pneumatic hammers in his body finally running out of steam. And in the silence, those quiet words pulse inside me, over and over: *Don't you understand? He will be great.*

But my own question pounds back: "How? How can someone so broken ever be great?"

From the time he was a baby, I'd spoken my father's words over Sam, the same nine words that Dad had said to me so often: *Remember, as you go through life, you're the greatest.*

I'd said it, but did I believe it? Greatness, here? The doctor at Children's Hospital — she said Sam would never grow out of it. The brain surgeon at UCLA — he said that Sam could be behind for life.

Don't you understand? He will be great.

Kneeling over Sam's bed in the stillness, those two phrases keep repeating in a quiet persistence like the soft tone of the homing beacon in Dad's old Cessna. My late father had explained it to me thirty years ago as we were bumping through the sky one day. It was the VOR, a radio beam in Morse code sent from small airports that helped him navigate his cross-country flights.

"As long as I hear that, John," Dad said, tapping the plane's dashboard, "we'll be fine. To stay on course, all I have to do is keep listening for that tone." When nothing below him looked familiar, he just kept listening for the beacon.

Don't you understand? He will be great.

I'm listening, Dad, but I don't understand. How will he ever be great?

PROLOGUE

Time, O Time, turn back in your flight
Make me a boy again just for tonight[1]

MY FATHER'S CONSTANT REFRAIN,
PARAPHRASING ELIZABETH AKERS ALLEN

THE STORYTELLER

My father loved to tell stories. Flanked by the kitschy wallpaper he'd hung in our Seventies kitchen, Dad would push himself back from the table, little Sarah would climb into his lap, and the gentle pace of his voice would transport my nine-year-old mind to Montana in the summer of 1945. The houndstooth pattern of the walls would give way to a dirty bus stop where I'd hear the soft bellow of the diesel and taste the gravel dust.

Dad, seventeen years old, stepped down from the Greyhound outside Yellowstone with two other high school friends, Rob and Hunter. Their hair slicked back in mild pompadours. T-shirts and dungarees smelling of the last pack of Lucky Strikes they'd burned through.

But as the bus rolled away down US 212, so did their prospects. That telegram they'd carried from Chicago was crumpled up and thrown to the ground: the promised summer job in the open air had gone to someone else. Rob folded his hand. Pulled out the bus schedule and found the next one back to Chicago. Dad and Hunter? They said they'd give it a go and soon found jobs washing dishes at the Roosevelt Lodge in Yellowstone. But Dad

19

hadn't come a thousand miles west to run cold water over congealed maple syrup.

After two weeks he'd had enough. Told Hunter he was quitting. They hitched a ride out of the park on a road grader, heading back to that bus stop. Creeping along the park road, Dad could already feel how slow the trip back to Chicago would be. His brother was shipping back from Europe, victorious over the Nazis. Dad was retreating from a stack of dishes.

The road-grader dropped Dad and Hunter at a diner near the northern gate of Yellowstone. Dad took one last shot. He stepped inside and asked the manager if anyone needed help for the summer. "Shorthill might," came the reply.

Mr. Shorthill turned on his diner stool and looked Dad over — my father at seventeen was not an impressive specimen. A hundred and a half. A skinny five-foot-nine. But the sheep rancher gave the city slickers a chance. And one of Dad's favorite stories was born.

Out the open windows of our kitchen, the lessening light smudged the greens and blacks of the shagbark hickories to gray.

As Sarah dropped off to sleep, Dad fingered his old coffee mug, conjuring memories over thirty years gone by. Of teenagers playing cowboy under the big sky. Of cold nights outside a warm cabin where, in the morning, Shorthill would wake Dad and Hunter by throwing rocks onto their tin roof with a *plink, plink.*

Down the long slope of our backyard, I could just start to see them. Points of luminescence glowed and dimmed, lit to the cadence of Dad's voice. Fireflies. I walked through our screen porch to stand on the patio and stare.

The whole world was slow dancing its way to bed. Beneath the trees, the soft yellow starlight went on and off, kissing the night with an unplaceable, perfect rhythm.

THE SUMMER AFTER FIFTH GRADE, I fell hard for a girl at camp. My bunkmate was dating her identical twin sister and I spent an infatuated week trying to figure out how to express that ours was the love of a lifetime.

At the camp gift shop, I plunked down the remainder of my spending money and bought her a small cross pendant. When the last day of camp came, I found her and her sister sitting on a picnic table, waiting for their parents. I sheepishly handed it to her, mumbling words I can't recall.

Her identical twin sister took the gift box from me and handed it to my love saying, "I think this is yours."

I had handed the necklace to the wrong girl. It was a mortification for the ages. But when I heard that she was going to return to camp for a later session that summer, I schemed to get back for a second week and a shot at redemption.

Coming home, I found my father reading the newspaper in his aqua blue easy chair with the clear plastic slipcovers. I sat down on the nearby piano bench and plucked up my courage.

"I met somebody at camp, Dad, and I really like her."

Without looking up from his newspaper, Dad said, "Well, it's really nice that you met a special friend."

Special friend? This woman — or someone who looked just like her — was my one-and-only!

And twenty-five years later when I called to tell him I was getting married, he once again missed the point.

Ever since I'd moved to California at the age of twenty-three, Dad started most phone conversations with some variation of the following:

"Is the car running? Do you need money? Okay, here's your mother." And if he felt mischievous he might add with a theatrical flourish: "Are you holding some maiden's hand?"

But that summer of 2005 when I rang Dad to tell him the news, he deviated from the script.

Lori and I were driving back from our engagement trip, a backpacking weekend through the high country of Yosemite. But Dad didn't want to hear the details of my proposal.

"Now, John, will you be needing the timeshare for your honeymoon?"

Let's see, Dad. I've just announced that after two decades of experiencing the exquisite delight of being the only single guy at family gatherings, I am finally being delivered. And your response is: *What about the timeshare?*

"Uh, Dad, we don't even have a date set for the wedding yet."

"Well, I'll need to know soon, John. Here's your mother."

A month or so later, I called my parents to tell them the wedding date.

"Have you decided what to do about the timeshare?" was the first question out of Dad's mouth. And the next call home was the same way. Exasperated, I came back at my father.

"Dad, I'm about to be married. You haven't said anything about what you think of Lori, any advice about marriage, about what you wish you would've done differently...."

"I'll tell you what I wish I would've done," he retorted. "I wish I would've planned my honeymoon!"

Then it all came back, another story of Dad's, their disastrous honeymoon night in the Smoky Mountains in 1955.

Dad had driven "straight through" as he liked to say, a good nine hours drive from Chicago. Undoubtedly, he'd made no reservations, but just motored around town as darkness fell, looking for a neon "Vacancy" sign.

They had dated for five years, trying to wear down Mom's mother. Mom was the good-girl Lutheran cheerleader. He was the leather jacket-wearing, ex-Army rogue, five years her elder. And worse, not just a Christian Scientist, but a lapsed one. (My grandmother might've accepted a heretic, but not one who wasn't serious about it.) Then, after some forbidden night of Northside slot-machines, he'd nearly killed her eldest daughter in his hopped up Mercury convertible by wrapping it around a telephone pole. I don't think Grandma ever gave her full-throated blessing, and he called her "Old Fats" — to her face — till the day she died.

But at last, on a brisk October evening, Shirley was his. The cabin they found outside the national park was modest, but who needs anything on this night of nights except a little love shack, right? Wrong — as Dad told it, tears in his eyes from laughing, the cabin's water heater clanged like a bell all night long.

Ah, the soundtrack of love.

And now, Dad was determined I wouldn't repeat his mistake. It had taken my whole life, but Dad and I were finally having "the talk."

The only other piece of relationship advice that Dad ever gave came to me indirectly, recalled by my older brother, Bob. When he was in his early twenties, he had gotten the straight scoop from Dad over the pool table in our basement.

23

"Bob," Dad began as he chalked his pool cue, "most guys get married to get inside a woman's pants."

Dad paused as he expertly lined up his bank shot.

"But you know what? Most people look better with their clothes on."

ABOUT A YEAR INTO OUR MARRIAGE, Lori sat me down at the kitchen table and drew a number line on a piece of notebook paper as if she was explaining integers to one of her high school students.

I was a C-minus math student.

"So, I ovulate ten days from my period," Lori began.

"For ten days after your period?" I asked.

"No, ten days *from* my period," she replied.

"That's what I said," I responded. Syntax must be to blame for some pregnancies.

She went back to the number line and counted ten days with her pencil, tap, tap, tap, from the first day of her period. "After which," she explained patiently, "I am ovulating for five to ten days."

No matter. One night a few months later, Lori lay down on the couch next to me and said that her tummy hadn't been feeling good.

"When did you have your period?" I asked.

"I can't remember," she replied.

"Maybe you're late."

"Well, you know, I'm always a little late," Lori said as she got up and went over to the kitchen calendar. "See," she said, "four weeks."

Lori may have gotten her masters in theology, but her calendar reading was Druid.

"What are you talking about? Count it again." It hadn't been four weeks. It had been six.

"Do you have a pregnancy test?" I asked.

"I think I have one lying around somewhere from The 99¢ Store."

Yep, ninety-nine cents. Because when Lori is discerning the outcome of life's most sacred act, that's the way she rolls.

And so it was that her first act the next morning was incongruously holy. Urine, announcing the formation of a soul. Pee, declaring: Glory to God in the highest.

Lori came out of the bathroom and lay down next to me on the bed. Neither of us could speak. Are there any words?

We stared at each other as silent as a cell dividing.

PART ONE
TAKEOFFS AND LANDINGS

Some beautiful sacred memory, preserved since childhood, is perhaps the best education of all. If a man carries many such memories into life with him, he is saved for the rest of his days. And even if only one good memory is left in our hearts, it may also be the instrument of our salvation one day.

FYODOR DOSTOYEVSKY

ONE
SIGNS OF LIFE

As I look at an ultrasound, my father is staring down a cardiograph.

I'm waiting for the first sign of life from my first child. And back in Chicago, after a few billion beats, Dad's old heart is finally acting its age.

In Pasadena, Lori and I squint at a little black and white screen that looks like an old TV set warming up for a game of Pong.

Lori's doctor squirts some gel onto her belly, pulls out what appears to be a karaoke microphone and plops it into the gel. Nearby, on the small black and white monitor, a vague outline of something is shape-shifting.

"So, here we can see the head," Dr. G. explains.

Head? What head? I say to myself.

I peer at the dark screen and see what appears to be Australia. But Lori nods and smiles, perfectly tracking. Wives have a bond with their OB's which is a bit unsettling.

"And here's the baby's back," Dr. G. continues, moving the karaoke mic down the side of her stomach.

Back?

"Mmmm," Lori says.

Dr. G. prods Lori's belly and Australia is now a large bean.

Congratulations, Dad-to-be, you're having a kidney. But first, we'd like you to take this Rorschach test brought to us by the folks at Atari.

I stare at the screen, deflated. I can't see a single, recognizable thing. Then Dr. G. turns up the volume. It's just static.

Then, coming through loud if not clear, is something fast and rhythmic:

Sh-Sh-Sh-Sh-Sh-Sh

My heartbeat quickens, racing as if to catch up.

The rapid fire sound is bold, brash, declarative. An audio tattoo. From inside a body I could've held in my palm, a muscle no bigger than a thimble is banging on the door of my heart, saying:

I'm here. Let me in. And I'll never leave.

Now Dr. G. is explaining the size of our baby's head. But all I can hear is this snare drum of a new soul.

Sh-Sh-Sh-Sh-Sh-Sh

What is this nameless ache? It's as close as my ribcage but just beyond my grasp.

What is it about hearing your baby's heartbeat for the first time?

In Puerto Rico, there's a radio telescope a thousand feet in diameter searching the sky for signs of life. We turn this stethoscope skyward. Scan the radio waves and look for clues. But all we've heard is "a faint hiss," as one pulsar scientist put it. A long whisper in the dark, collapsing stars sending the same signature, over and over.

And now there's this ping from deep space, inches away, but shrouded in the dark of Lori's belly.

From their first trimester, our children are casting a rope on our dock. They come from a place of mystery to our safe harbor and then cast off so soon, back out to sea. In an instant, we see it all before us. And its grandeur seeps through our eyes in a speechless language of tears.

BACK IN CHICAGO, it's a different story. A great heart, a heart like no other I'd ever known, sends a distress call. The snare drum is offbeat and the sticky leads stuck to Dad's skin tell the tale: the cardiograph records diminishing electrical charges. The ping from deep space has grown a little faint. Dad's doctor says he'll need a quintuple bypass.

Even though our family had seen it coming for years — the "spells," falling off the ladder, trouble climbing stairs — it was difficult for any of us to imagine Dad fading. All my life he'd moved with certainty and speed. At wedding receptions, he'd spin Mom like a carnival ride and she'd turn and return, sure and shining.

When I call him with our news, I can tell he's winded. But that can't dampen his enthusiasm.

"Oh, well done, John," he gets out, waiting for his next breath. "And if it's a boy, there's a chance to carry on the line!" After eight grandchildren from my sisters, Dad still didn't have a grandson who bore his last name.

And then, perhaps feeling his own racing heart, he says, "John, it's good you're having a child, because when you're old, someone will take care of you."

TWO

THE HOUSE ACROSS THE STREET
FROM THE CEMETERY

My father's surgery takes place in Lori's first trimester, and I fly back to Chicago to help with his recovery. I take the night shift at the hospital and read aloud to him.

I listen to the space between the electronic beeps from the machine near Dad's bed. Like the ticking of a grandfather clock, his seventy-nine-year-old heart seems to slow but never stop.

My father knew all about pumps and keeping things flowing. For almost forty years, Dad had built and sold systems throughout industrial Chicago designed to move fresh water onto jetliners, recover used ink from newspaper presses, and a hundred other things.

As he drops off to sleep, his hospital bed is incongruous with the blur of motion that had been his life: finding joy in getting his pilot's license, vacationing from Yellowstone to the Grand Canyon, and building his own homes.

In 1970, shortly after the birth of my little sister, Dad bought an undeveloped acre of land an hour from Chicago, with oak trees rising from a gentle slope. The first house Dad had built fifteen years earlier in Skokie was bursting at the seams with four kids on a tiny lot. Like his ranching days in Montana, Dad wanted room for us to roam.

For the next two years, he and Mom designed their dream home and Dad spent weekends and evenings as the general contractor, slowly building it with handpicked guys, doing much of the work himself.

And if he ever gave a thought to building my childhood home across the street from a cemetery, he never mentioned it. I never knew my father to be afraid of anything. Certainly not the dead.

My bedroom window looked out on Assumption Cemetery and its meandering driveway: almost a mile of crumbling pavement in the shape of a potato. Most of the headstones didn't even peek above the grass. It was just an open field with a forest on its north, a cornfield to its back, and our street, Winfield Road, running along the front.

But in my father's curating, the graveyard was a flight deck and launch pad, a runway and drag strip. It was an imaginary South Pole with fearless explorers. And silent witness to a childhood filled with bellowing tractors and screaming snowmobiles.

I close my eyes and like a Polaroid being peeled open in my father's hands, everything comes back in high contrast color.

THREE
MAIL ORDER SHOES AND
CLIP-ON TIES

My father had a style all his own. Visiting his work, I remember him bounding up the stairs from the machine shop to the cigarette-scented sales office, waltzing in the door, and raising one arm in mockery of his tour of duty in postwar Italy.

"No saluting, men, not necessary," he'd say to his fellow salesmen. But they all knew the truth behind his playful brio. It sat on the ring finger of his right hand: nine diamonds set in the company logo, each one symbolizing a million-dollar year. When a million dollars still meant something.

When I would come up from the warehouse, he'd sit bent over his desk engulfed by half-filled order sheets, the old Bell touchtone propped on one shoulder. Hanging on the wall would be his beloved aviation calendar, which he gave as Christmas gifts to clients. Emblazoned on the bottom was custom printed: *Semler Industries, Skills in Handling Solutions, Franklin Park, Illinois.*

Dad would put down the phone, turn to me and say, "I feel like a mosquito in a nudist camp, I don't know where to strike first."

The clothes he bought were never used but they were made of

unknown materials. To wit, Dad's beloved mail order shoes from Haband, size nine. He was so proud of those fake leather knockoffs — three pairs for twenty-one dollars. When they'd come in the parcel post, he'd open the box with a sense of occasion, pulling them from the wrapping as if he was unpacking a crate of exotic taxidermy at the Field Museum.

He'd hold up the dress loafers with their faux gold clasp, immediately put them on, and march around the kitchen glorying in their synthetic perfection, pumping his fists up and down at his sides like two pistons.

They were startlingly impervious to wear and tear as he strode through solvents and muck. But after absorbing the fumes of refineries, they'd no longer hold their shine and be too battered even for Dad's frugal fashion sense.

They'd be retired to the garage where Dad would slip them on to mow the lawn or squeegee black driveway sealant in the fall. Finally, they'd be too encrusted with the dreck of asphalt and grass clippings to be worn by even him. And it's probably inaccurate to speak of them in the past tense; decades later they are undoubtedly still intact, buried beneath strata of landfill. If archeologists ever unearth them, the fashion sense of The Seventies Salesman will be a marvel of incorruptibility.

And my father was incorruptible. Old Nebuchadnezzar may have seen the frightful vision of the statue with the feet of clay, but my father stood tall in those damn shoes which couldn't possibly have been comfortable as he walked briskly through the machine shop, barking encouragement. Not with those socks anyway. Dad would wear them through till his big toenail would peek out like a half moon, and then switch that sock to the other foot hoping that pinky toe wouldn't get the same bright idea. Mom had to beg him to throw away those brown and black polyester hose. But, God as my witness, he'd cover the new hole with masking tape and keep wearing them.

His neckties were a category unto themselves but not for their patterns which were just muted diagonals. What set them apart was that each one was, to the last, a clip-on. And why not? Why mess with tying a Windsor? The clip-on, after all, kept its perfect shape, just like his shoes. Unchanged by the weather of Chicago or the climate of fashion, that inverted triangle perched perfectly beneath his button-down Oxford collar for decades.

But never for long. Ever the pragmatist and mindful that he was around machinery, Dad would fling it into the backseat of his Impala company car, where the ties of that week would pile up like thick fettuccine.

FOUR
THE RACE FOR THE GATE

In the fading heat of summer sunsets, my father, little sister, and I rode bikes together around the loop of Assumption Cemetery. Sarah on her high-riser, me on my Huffy with its fake plastic gas tank, and Dad on his blue Schwinn Collegiate five-speed that probably weighed a hundred pounds.

As we circled the loop, the excitement would build. I knew what was coming; our final route was always the same. After completing the circle, we'd turn down the long, wide driveway that bisected the cemetery.

We both knew, hearts racing, that Dad would give us a head start.

Maybe this time will be different. Such are the things you tell yourself as a child.

From far behind us Dad would shout, "It's a race for the gate!" and our legs would begin to pedal furiously.

We'd shoot down the straightaway, aiming dead ahead for the front gate, a hundred yards away.

beat him? Can they beat him?" he'd shout from
us. And as I heard his words, I thought anything was
ble. Even beating my father in a bike race.

Our legs were burning, dying. We're both screaming, laughing,
because we knew, we knew: it wasn't going to be enough for
Dad to pass us, nor merely streak by.

No, he had to do it with style.

We looked over our shoulders and he'd be gaining on us.
Serenely. Pedaling that iron Schwinn in fifth gear, like he didn't
have a care in the world.

As he came up on us, his hands would be off the handlebars, his
arms moving as if he was jogging in slow motion. He'd go by
smoothly, not saying a word. Just grinning, his arms pumping.

And those beat-up fake leather shoes moving like the winged
feet of Mercury.

FIVE

SNOWMOBILE CPR

The winter of 1978 and '79 had a blizzard that lasted for days. Drifts covered our window sills. Snow plows piled masses into mountains a dozen feet high.

We luxuriated in five full snow days of no school. No homework. And nothing to do except make our way across the street to Assumption Cemetery and bury ourselves.

In front of the graveyard, the drainage ditch running along Winfield Road had created snowdrifts far taller than our fifth grade bodies. Diving in, we dug a sprawling underground igloo.

The neighbor kid and I pawed deeper and deeper, and our tunnels went on into the depths. We dug rooms, magically lit, white and translucent. We were no longer in the suburbs. We were in a cave in the Alps fighting Nazis. Or somewhere in Narnia. Anything was possible. Because a minute before, it had not existed at all.

At night, my sister and I nestled alongside Dad as he read to us an eclectic mix of history, nature stories, and economics — the life of the grizzly bear, the duel between Burr and Hamilton, and that venerable essay of free market orthodoxy, *I, Pencil.*

But one thing that winter was the same as it ever was — Dad's cold weather fashion sense.

The stocking cap was a beige rayon, pilled with use. The overcoat was whichever one had gotten too stained from the last sales call. And the boots were black rubber and calf-high, with a zipper down the middle the way God and Kmart intended. Dad would shove his shoes into plastic baggies and down into those waterproof wonders, and then stomp off to the garage to practice CPR on the snowmobile.

Dad rarely bought anything new. Dogs, horses, tractors, and a cantankerous snowmobile were all bought used and on the cheap. My older sister had finally gotten her pony, Andy, a nag with undiagnosed worms who refused to gallop. The dog, a castoff poodle from some acquaintance, was a neurotic who followed my mother everywhere. The snowmobile outlasted them both.

But before each new season, the desiccated Ski-Doo was in need of a defibrillator. Sitting outside for one more Chicago summer, it had grown a mint-green fuzz over the battery leads.

Outside, between pulls on the rip-cord starter, I could hear Dad trying the electric ignition. I walked into the garage to find him engulfed in blue-gray smoke that sweetened the air with two-cycle oil. The snowmobile's engine groaned, turning over like a drunk in a dream.

The front clamshell of the snowmobile was tilted forward exposing the engine and some jacked up fiberglass repair. At some point before Dad bought it, the front end had been shattered against a pole or a pine. It looked like it was held together with yellowed Scotch tape.

I peered into the side of the engine housing, wondering how it worked. Mechanical things were a mystery to me, and Dad wasn't much of a teacher.

"John," he said, "I need you to hold this can and shoot it ... right" — Dad grabbed my arm like it was a draftsman's lamp, firmly adjusting the spray can of Go-Start into position — "shoot it right ... there." With the nozzle finally aimed correctly, Dad mounted the seat and turned the key.

As the battery lazily labored the pistons into action, Dad would yell, "Now, John, now!"

As whatever I was spraying doused the spark plug, something moved up and down inside the cylinders with an argumentative clang and finally surrendered, spitting percussive barks and coughing smoke in complaint.

By then it was night, but Dad wasn't about to let a finally live engine go to waste.

"Get on, John Boy!" he yelled above the cold clamor.

I hopped on the cold, stiff vinyl seat behind Dad and wrapped my arms around his waist. Dad flipped on the headlight, we exited our driveway, and I heard a scrape as Dad steered the Ski-Doo over the asphalt of our street, and back onto the snow in the drainage ditch on the other side.

Then the beast leapt forward as if towed by a comet. I grabbed at Dad's waist, tighter and tighter, as he roared toward the cemetery and the fields beyond.

SIX
THE MOTHER OF ALL CHILD-BIRTHING CLASSES

Watch any film involving childbirth made during my father's generation and you'll likely see a dad in the waiting room of a hospital, smoking a cigarette. And in 1958, that's probably where you would've found my father, waiting for news on his firstborn, my older sister, Sherry. A Lucky Strike in one hand and the *Chicago Tribune* in the other, Dad scanning the editorial page to see if they'd published one of his letters.

Ah, the enlightened dads of this century. Our dads paced the floor, but at ten paces we can spot "false labor." At parties with other dads, we debate the merits of epidurals like we're starting a new wide receiver in fantasy football. It's a fantasy, all right. "Oh, sure," I say at a baby shower somewhere, "we thought about having a doula, but Lori thinks I can handle it." Yes, midwife is my middle name.

Lori signs us up for a natural child-birthing class, which only reinforces my delusion. About a dozen dads and moms sit in a circle around a living room on Sunday nights and for ten weeks we learn about natural childbirth from Momma K. — midwife, educator, and one-woman medical-establishment wrecking-crew.

I take notes, ask questions, and try to memorize the stuff I'm going to need to know for the big day. Because if I don't, Momma K. strongly implies, I'm going to kill my baby.

Because if Lori's doctor is cowed by malpractice lawsuits, then all that stands in the way of a proper, "natural" labor is me, The Birth Coach. That day, as she works her way through contractions, only I can stop injections of these Make-the-Baby-Come-Faster drugs.

If I don't monitor the fetal monitor, my precious baby will be bombarded with radio waves, sonar waves, and may never be able to do The Wave at a Chicago Bears game.

And if I don't spend hundreds of dollars on a Swiss-made breast pump, then I should seriously question my broader purpose in the universe.

But my purpose, as it turns out, is learning one salient item — when do we leave for the hospital? Thus, I memorize "4-1-1," which will mean that Lori's contractions are:

- Four minutes apart
- Are lasting for one minute
- And have been like that for one hour

That is when we take off.

Whoa — you got that? I, The Dad, have a ROLE. No, this is more than a role. This is, writ large, the intrinsic law of a happy marriage: knowing what your wife wants from you.

So 4-1-1 is my new mantra. I repeat it to co-workers. I'm like a preschooler who's just learned to count. My single guy-friends listen and nod blankly, wondering when the conversation might turn back to football.

ONE NIGHT, Momma K. has us practice "reflective breathing," lying on our sides facing our wives and breathing when they breathe. The whole room sounds like beached whales at low tide. And then the screaming started. From me.

Momma K. suggests that the dads get some small idea of how much pain the moms will be in. The moms like this idea very much, and we dads look at each other like the cornered wimps we are. Because here is the Unwritten Rule of Childbearing: one of you is going to be in pain and one of you is not. And the gender who is *not* in said pain should feel guilty about the accident of a chromosome which has let our gender romp through history inventing glass ceilings, the *Sports Illustrated* swimsuit issue, and patriarchy itself.

The penance she has in mind seems harmless. Momma K. passes out ice-cubes and tells the dads to hold onto one cube for ninety seconds, while relaxing, breathing, whatever: I couldn't hear what she is saying because of an exquisite, burning-yet-freezing sensation of —

"Oh-my-freaking-GOSH that is COLD," I blurted out after fifteen seconds.

Here I am, trying to hold one rock of a shot glass and writhing in pain. "To the woman He said, 'I will greatly multiply your pain in childbirth....'" Labor contractions are the original Act of God.

I'm also deluded into overconfidence from all the homework. Momma K. drills the Dads over and over. I start to feel book-smart. But I can't stave off my deeper emotions. As Lori waddles through the last trimester, the birth feels like a tsunami, something unstoppable headed our way. As much as the class includes me and gives me a role somewhere between cheer-leader and masseuse, there is no getting around this ominous sense that something is fundamentally out of my control.

Still, Momma K. makes it sound like Dads are, well, a flight traffic controller. Not flying the plane, of course, but bringing that baby in for a landing.

Ah, no. I am the baggage handler. And this tiny person who doesn't yet exist will require two suitcases which could hold eight babies fully clothed. Luggage that will be packed and repacked several times and stored in the car for weeks. Because that baby is going to land, like all babies, right in the middle of whatever night it chooses.

Every aspect of this says the same thing: life is not of my bidding. In my career, in courtship, and now with "deciding to have a baby," I've told myself that results were due to my initiative.

But who am I kidding? My career kept twisting and turning into blessings I didn't deserve. And Lori — beautiful, sweet Lori? No one, least of all me, could understand why this doll of grace had chosen me. I knew me. Me was pretty freaking weird. A little manic. Half-depressed, half the time. Yet here she was, at long last. And I knew I hadn't called her love into being. It was, as the old theologians say, unmerited favor.

No, a child's arrival on the planet is like being invited to a surprise party. You're not sure when the guest of honor will arrive. So try to stay quiet. Like most parties, you've been asked to go to this one by your wife. Not because you're necessary, but because it would be nice to have you around.

My own father's declining health should be a stark reminder that life is not of my choosing. Yet deeply ingrained in me is a long list of assumptions about how my child's life will go from here. He will walk and talk on schedule. He will ride a bike. Have rich friendships. And one day, will launch out on his own.

But these are just illusions. And in the next few years, like most illusions, they will vanish before my eyes.

SEVEN
SCULPTURES OF STEEL

The year after he graduated from high school, Dad tried to enlist in the Air Force but was refused — he was colorblind. And years later when Dad finally got his pilot's license, the wisdom of that Air Force recruiter came into stark relief. Even at small airports like ours, pairings of red and white runway lights shine upward to let pilots know if they're coming in too steeply. One day, just seconds before landing, Dad leaned over and yelled above the Lycoming engine, "John, are those lights down there red or white?" No wonder my mother wasn't enthusiastic about the hobby.

At the age of eight, Dad made a deal with me. If I read *We*, the autobiography of Charles Lindbergh, he would give me five dollars, a small fortune in 1976. When I completed that, he and I subscribed to the Military Book Club and Christmas came every month. When one of those big flat cardboard boxes arrived, I would climb into my top bunk and read about boys over Borneo and Berlin, kids barely out of high school gripping .50-caliber machine guns and lining up swastikas in their crosshairs.

If those books were my liturgy, then Oshkosh was our cathedral. Every year as July turned to August, one of the largest air shows on earth packed the Wisconsin sky with every imaginable plane, from the Concorde to motorized parachutes. Before dawn on the big day, Dad would pull back my Western print bedspread and give me a back rub with his knuckles till I stirred.

Downstairs in the darkened kitchen, the blender would be going, mixing up the powdered protein shake that Dad made us drink every morning. As a child raised during a time of scarcity, Dad probably thought it the height of indulgence when he added a banana to the froth, but that only made me hate the fruit for years thereafter. The only way I could stifle my gag reflex was to drink the chalky brew in one gulping heave and immediately stuff a Pop-Tart into my mouth.

Breakfast thus endured, I climbed into the front seat of Dad's massive Chevy Impala and we took off into the misty morning, up the empty two-lane of Route 59 and into the verdant green of the dairy state. Passing through Fon du Lac on Interstate 41, Dad and I craned our necks out the windows to catch a glimpse of what we were beginning to hear: the twelve-cylinder vibrato of that hot rod of the war, the P-51 Mustang.

We pulled into Wittman Field and marveled. Across dozens of grassy acres were parked hundreds of time machines: decades old and nearly priceless, the planes from my books sat there on the grass, touchable, sculptures of steel with names like Thunderbolt, Corsair, and Lightning. I ran my hands over the rivets and poked my fingers into the gun barrels.

Then, Dad and I carried our aluminum folding chairs with the crosshatched nylon along the flightline and set them down in front of the runway. And then came the real shock: Dad, who never allowed anything but tap water at restaurants, bought me a cold Coca-Cola and we settled into our seats for the show.

The Marines' mighty Harrier jet hovered like a helicopter.

An aerobatic champion took his plane straight up and then flew backwards, falling tail-first towards earth, hanging on the prop.

And one of my heroes, Bob Hoover — who had escaped from a POW camp by stealing a German fighter — flew the wings off a Shrike Commander. The Shrike was, mind you, a business plane. A twin-prop puddle jumper. But physics be damned: if you can swipe a plane from the Nazis, what can't you do?

Bob turned the engines completely off. The crowd went utterly still. The only sound was the wind going past his wings as he came swooping down on the deck "dead-stick," his propellers stopped. And then he looped it high into the sky and silently back down before us. I could've died happy, right there.

Down the flightline, someone climbed into a Hellcat. There was an electric whine as the starter coerced eighteen pistons into action, fighting vacuum and compression. The fourteen-foot propeller turned majestically as oxygen and fuel were drawn into cylinders the size of my second-grade torso. And then the engine erupted with a sound like bowling balls being shaken in oil drums. It taxied for takeoff like a 1940s newsreel, and then sailed steeply into the sky.

Making a wide circuit, it barrel rolled past us at 300 mph, the nylon crosshatch sticking to the back of my t-shirt, the Coke rolling down my throat, and Dad pointing his Super 8 movie camera to the sky, the back of his neck farmer tanned like cherry wood.

AFTER THE SHOW WRAPPED UP, Dad and I walked wearily back to the Chevy, windburned and hearts full. Somewhere along the Interstate I got sleepy and put my head in his lap. As I dropped off, Dad asked me what had been my favorite part of the day.

I think I mumbled, "Mustang." Or maybe I said, "Coca-Cola."

Then I drifted off into a dreamland of dogfights over dairy farms, past cumulus clouds against a silken blue.

EIGHT

THE WINTER CAMPAIGN

Throughout the summer and fall the baby grows in Lori's belly and Dad makes progress in his rehab, faithfully showing up for cardio therapy and tramping the treadmill for all he's worth. His clothes fit more loosely now, but there's still a spark in his eye. A defiant pilot light still glows in his furnace.

And then one day that winter, everything changes. Dad stretches a dollar to breaking point and it breaks him.

Mom and Dad had been buying timeshares. And every year, Dad has to use the points or they'll expire. So just six months after his bypass surgery and over our protests, Dad gets Mom and him onto a plane for Branson, Missouri — in December.

A week later, a call comes from the hospital there: *your Dad has collapsed and is dying. Get here as soon as you can.*

I mutter through prayers as I pack, stopping to lean on the condo wall and cry. Odd reflections come up out of nowhere: I realize that it's Pearl Harbor Day and I think how Dad would've appreciated the symmetry — his own surprise attack. But I go right back to crying as I realize that he might never meet my baby, due next month. We'd planned to fly home next year during Lori's spring break. He'd been so excited lately, insisting that it was a girl.

I land in Springfield, Missouri, and stand shivering outside the airport, looking through the blistering wind at the dead grass. It's the last place any sane person would go on a winter vacation. Unless that person was a child of the Great Depression who would feel abject guilt at having wasted his timeshare points.

The four of us kids gather in Dad's hospital room. I hug Mom but her arms are loose around me. She used to hug me so tight when I'd come to visit, was so exuberant, so excited that I was home. But the dementia of the past five years has been a thief, making off with her joy and passion.

She sits down, not next to Dad's bed, but in a corner of the room. Her face is muted, neither sunshine nor sorrow. She knows something is amiss, but the moment doesn't adhere.

The doctor explains that Dad had a "hemorrhagic event" on his brain, a kind of stroke which caused a fall in the bathroom of their timeshare. The housekeeping crew found Dad unconscious a couple of hours later. And Mom, sitting on the bed, unaware of what had happened.

We try to talk to Dad, tell him we're here, but he fades in and out, coming to then slipping away. It's touch and go through that weekend. But then, to the surprise of the staff, Dad rallies. His doctor says he could make the trip back to Chicago this coming week.

I'm between freelance jobs and tell my brother and sisters that I can stay with Dad till he's ready. They fly back north with Mom, but she's never far from his thoughts. He spends most of the afternoon in a mild delirium, asking about her. He tells me to make sure she has one of his protein shakes. He says there's orange juice in the fridge. I listen into the night and then, exhausted, head back to my hotel.

I wake to a freezing rain that lacquers the windshield of my car. I pass a nativity crèche standing wet in front of a gas station, missing its set dressing of snow.

In Dad's room, carols from Johnny Mathis and Bing Crosby warble through the tinny speaker. He wakes, the rain on the windowsill combining with the carols to mix up his mind; he tells me to "put some logs on the fire, the logs in the garage are dry." I stroke his hair and he falls back to sleep.

I get word that the weather has grounded the ambulance jet that was scheduled to take Dad back to Chicago. I sit down next to his bed, pull out one of his World War II books about the Battle of the Bulge, and read to him.

The Nazis have encircled Bastogne. Howitzer shells shriek down, sending a murderous hail of shrapnel and snow through the desperate troops. The same brutal winter that Dad's brother endured in Belgium comes alive. Helpless at his HQ in Luxembourg, General Patton strides into the chapel, kneels under the crucifix, and addresses God in a blunt and brutal psalm of complaint.

> Sir, this is Patton talking. The last fourteen days have been
> straight hell. Rain, snow, more rain, more snow — and I'm begin-
> ning to wonder what's going on in Your headquarters. Whose side
> are You on, anyway?

Outside Dad's hospital room, rainy ice pelts the black windowpane. As I read, his beautiful hazel eyes flutter open and close again. He comes to, seems to know that I'm here, and then dozes off. How many times as a child did I fall asleep to the sound of his reading? More than the stars in the sky.

I'VE BEEN in Missouri for almost a week. I'm coming down with something and am weary beyond words. As I check out of my hotel room, the housekeeper mentions that she's praying for Dad. Then she looks at me with unaccountable warmth and says, "You will go out with joy and be led forth with peace."[2]

The sun comes out. I walk into Dad's room and he greets me by name, which he hasn't done all week. I grasp his hand, and tell him that he's finally going to get to fly on a private jet. Dad is woozy, but squeezes my hand. I tell him that I really want to fly with him but that he's going to have to do this one without me. He gives me a thumbs up.

The next day, the jet makes its final descent to Dad's home field, DuPage County Airport. And if the medical pilot happens to look off to the right, past the McMansions, he might see what Dad always pointed out to me: Assumption Cemetery and our home.

After we'd take off in that old Cessna, he'd let me take the controls. We'd bounce along at a thousand feet, and I would look down on that driveway where we rode our bikes. Dad would take back the yoke and waggle the wings back and forth like some fighter pilot buzzing a field in jolly old England.

Now the old ace was on approach to his home base. Shot up, but not yet out of the fight.

NINE
SACRED MYOPIA

As Lori and I tour the labor and delivery ward near Pasadena, Dad goes in and out of the ICU back in Chicago. He's released only to return, every recovery followed by a setback. We talk on the phone. He's there, trying to track with me, but disoriented. Not himself.

On January 26, Lori's early contractions start. It's 4:30 p.m. on a Wednesday when she calls me at the office. "It feels like the uterus is giving the baby a hug!" she says.

Yeah? I think, *Fidel Castro hugged people, too.*

The next morning, Lori says the pain has gotten worse. I follow her around our condo complex like a lost puppy. At the onset of a contraction, she turns, throws her right arm around my neck, holds up her belly with her left, and squats down while telling me to stand up straight. She makes a deep, guttural hum like she's smelling a newly made In-N-Out burger.

My vertebrae feel like a pogo stick at a fat camp. I feel useful, but that feeling quickly fades; just as she gets a good squat going, Lori pushes me away, moaning.

I pull out my spiral notebook and study the numbers I've been jotting down, looking for the revered 4-1-1 pattern. But Lori's contractions are as predictable as a hummingbird on RedBull.

At about 2:30 p.m., I do the math for the umpteenth time. I've got 4-1-1. I get Lori into the car.

We arrive at the hospital, Lori quickly dilates to eight centimeters and then — nothing. Her water won't break. Lori recalls something from class — what was it? — about not breaking the water artificially. Like a nerd, I quickly consult my class notes and announce: "Urine is yellow and smells and tastes like urine."

Uh, no — that is how you know a bladder has emptied, not that water has broken. I'm in the deep end now. I try calling Momma K., but she's taken her daughter to see a Broadway production of *Wicked*.

Lori is resolute. She's come this far with no IV, no pain meds, nothing. She's determined to climb this mountain the same way she summited all 14,505 feet of Mount Whitney. But she's in pain. Dr. G. comes in and sits down on the bed next to Lori.

"What are you afraid of, Lori?" he asks. Lori shares that she wants a completely natural childbirth. Dr. G. explains that the water could stay unbroken for hours and — naturally — hours from now, she'll be too tired to push.

We decide to break the water, and immediately energy shoots through the room. Lori's body is wracked by what appears to be an alien force. Now my cheat sheet is truly worthless. The last notes to myself sound so stupid:

Remind Lori to:
* *listen to her body*
* *push with her abdomen not her face*

"Listen to her body"? Every nerve in her body is bellowing. She's not exhaling slowly. And she most definitely is pushing with her face — I barely recognize her face.

Do you critique an artist at her canvas? Do you interrupt a Eucharist? No. This is holy ground. Labor and Delivery is now a church.

So I throw away the cheat sheet and wipe Lori's face with a cold washcloth. I whisper encouragement. I watch her in awe. I cheer her on. But of course, I may as well not be there. Because Lori is utterly focused. She has shoved everything else aside in a holy myopia.

I steal a glance and can see the top of Sam's head, dark strands of hair on a wet billiard ball. And then *whump!* Dr. G. pulls Sammy into the waiting world.

I shout, "Lori, you did it, you did it!"

"Next time," she says in exhaustion, "I'm scheduling a C-section."

I cut the cord. He's wiped down and put in a receiving blanket. She gathers him to her. And, with nary a cry, he peacefully sets the side of his head against her breast. He's home.

How could a whole person just be here, when a minute ago he wasn't? Sam had spent the last nine months just inches away, but it's like he's arrived from another planet.

His mere existence feels so lavish, so wildly indulgent. How can something so obviously miraculous be given to two normal, run-of-the-mill people like us?

I take him in my arms and say, "You're here, you're here, you're finally here!"

I CALL Dad with the news. "His name is Sam, Dad. You finally have a grandson with your last name. His middle name is Robert, Dad, your name."

I can tell he's happy for me but his wit seems submerged, his mind held under the waves of whatever happened on that cold day at the timeshare two months ago.

I try to explain that we're also giving Lori's Irish forebears a little love with a second middle name, Aedan.

Dad's not too sure about that. Two middle names? It probably strikes him as very Californian. "The land of fruits and nuts," he'd often call my adopted state. But even in his exhaustion, he can't keep that curve of moxie out of his voice.

"Well, *Robert*, that's an outstanding name, John."

TEN
HERE'S LOOKING AT YOU, KID

Sam won't look at me.

Lori says that Sam recognizes my voice. That when I walk into the room while he's nursing, he pauses, his eyes darting back and forth.

But when I hold him, Sam looks away. I put him on my knee to burp him and he looks everywhere but into my eyes.

Yes, I'm expecting the etiquette of eye contact from a two-week-old. From a baby whose eyesight is good for twelve inches. But I've waited so long to see him. I want him to wave back. And I don't have lactating breasts, the ultimate in self-validating equipment.

There's no exhaustion like newborn parenting. You would willingly commit felony crime to have the child sleep more than two hours. In this death march, the nursing breast stands alone. It can do no wrong. It gets the little bug to sleep, but it leaves dads high and dry. Even during pregnancy, I had felt closer to Embryo Sam than Two-Week-Old Sam. The mighty breast is having more face time with my son than I am.

Lori is quick to tell me that nursing is not interpersonal ecstasy. What she's enduring through dazed nights and time-sucking days is largely mechanical. More Bondo than bonding. But, romantic to the last, I go looking for connection.

But Sam is going to reveal himself on his terms and in his timing.

HE'S three weeks old now. Lori is bushed and I tell her that I'll put him down. I shut the door and remember something from class. I try to fool Sam by putting my pinky finger upside down in his mouth and rocking him.

But Sam is having none of this neo-nipple. He spits out my finger like a wad of Red Man from the first inning. Then becomes almost frantic as he realizes that it's just Daddy's finger, not the soft-serve he's used to.

Then I remember this CD I got from Lori. The producer had traveled around to air shows recording old airplanes. I put it on and feather the volume knob as the track starts. Quietly filling the room is a sound of faraway airplanes, like distant bumblebees.

Sam stops crying. He takes my little finger back in his mouth and starts sucking.

The planes sound closer now. I look at the CD cover. It's a recording of the Reno Air Races at Pylon 6, where fighter planes pass overhead at 400 mph, their wings set in a vertical knife-edge. I remember reading about these races as a kid. This is going to get loud.

It happens — there's a wonderful Doppler effect as the planes scream by. Our stereo's speakers bleed the sound from right to left. Sam eyes look back and forth as if to say, *What did I just hear?* Then he goes back to sucking.

The next track on the CD sounds voyeuristic. There's so much ambient noise, it feels like we're in the hangar. The hum of the starter begins. I can almost smell the engine oil as it simmers. And then it roars out the exhaust manifold in puffs of white smoke.

I look down. Sam is falling asleep to the sound of 4,000 horsepower. It taxis away, the engine's thumping cadence fades. Sam's breathing gets regular, and then, with a big exhale, he falls asleep.

The next day I try the same CD again — and it works. Is the sound of airplanes going to be our thing, like it was with Dad and me?

But the next night, Sam doesn't go for it. It's Mommy milk or nothing.

And through it all, Sam won't look at me.

I could not know it then, but Sam was introducing me to a way of relating that would be set to his own rhythm. Even as he looked everywhere but into my eyes, he was carving his unspoken language into the soft tissue of my heart. Relationship, I would slowly realize over the next several years, would be on his terms.

The week goes by. Sam turns a month old. I'm holding him one day and he looks at me. He catches my eye and holds it. For the first time.

Two weeks later, Dad will be gone.

ELEVEN
TAKING FLIGHT

Sam turns six weeks old and I get an urgent call from my sister. Dad is in hospice, going fast.

I curse my lack of foresight. Why didn't I get on a plane weeks ago? Why didn't I give Dad a chance to meet his new grandson?

I just didn't think he was going to die. I believed one more of Dad's nine lives was going to spring to life. Just as he had done five times in the past four months, I thought he'd leave ICU, and head back to rehab where he had been making decent, if erratic, improvement.

By the time we arrive in Chicago, Dad has slipped out of consciousness. I lay Sammy in his arms, but Dad doesn't stir. Sam can't even keep his head up, but for some reason reaches up towards Dad's face and touches his grandfather's chest. It rises and falls under his tiny hand, laboring for breath.

My father's cheeks are still ruddy. His hair, still full, white and beautifully soft.

I hold his hand. I tell him thank you. I thank him for showing me how to be a man. And for giving me a childhood filled with wonder.

We sing one of his favorite songs, "Great is Thy Faithfulness," hoping he can hear; we've been told that hearing is one of the last senses to leave. And then all of us, except my little sister, Sarah, go back to the house to sleep.

In the middle of the night, Sarah stirs where she's napping at the hospice and feels like she should go to Dad's room. She steals to my father's bedside, opens the Psalms and reads aloud:

> *Bless the Lord, O my soul,*
> *And all that is within me, bless His holy name.*
> *Bless the Lord, O my soul,*
> *And forget none of His benefits;*
> *Who pardons all your iniquities,*
> *Who heals all your diseases;*
> *Who redeems your life from the pit,*
> *Who crowns you with lovingkindness and compassion;*
> *Who satisfies your years with good things,*
> *So that your youth is renewed like the eagle.* [3]

As Sarah read the word "eagle," Dad took a deep breath. It was his last.

My father, as was his habit, took flight.

TWELVE
REMEMBER, YOU'RE THE GREATEST

My parents' church has all the reverence of a truck stop. Inside, the squat dome is held up by two long arches that cross in the middle. Garish lights in glass globes light the place with a Vegas glare. It's modern, yet already dated. Not timeless like my father.

But the mood is rescued, as usual, by Dad. As I take the podium, I glance up from my notes. The deep love he had for people looks back in a mosaic of faces, glazed with wet eyes, glowing with memory.

"Remember, as you go through life, you're the greatest," I begin, recounting one of my father's phrases. I'd heard him say those nine words throughout my life, but the repetition hadn't dimmed its power — nor uncovered its mystery.

It was mysterious because Dad had high standards. People were to be respected for their character; "by their fruits you'll know them," he'd often say. The importance he placed on valor and courage came through every time he introduced me to an old fighter pilot. When I was a kid, I remember coming into our darkened family room one night to find Dad lost in reverie, his old hi-fi crackling as he played a speech on LP — Douglas MacArthur's farewell address to West Point, *Duty, Honor, Country.*

So, what Dad thought was great was clear. But regularly and often, he inverted this scale of achievement. He turned it on its head. Again and again, a blessing was spoken over me without any kind of accomplishment attached to it. In fact, without anything attached to it whatsoever. We were kids, we hadn't achieved anything at all, and yet — "Remember, as you go through life, you're the greatest."

He said it when dropping us off for a sleepover. After moving the last box into my college dorm room. And when saying goodbye at the airport.

Dad never explained those words. And as I work my way through my eulogy, I put a question to his friends and colleagues.

"What could it mean?" I ask the hundreds who'd come to see Dad off. "After all, we can't all be the greatest, can we? I mean, if he said it to me," I joke, "how could he have meant it for you?" Looking out on the crowd, I see some acknowledging smiles; they'd heard him say it to them, too. They'd felt his spirited belief in them.

There is, of course, no explaining this outlandish statement that a little boy hears from the time he can walk, that he hears nearly every time he leaves the house, and that echoes through the canyons of his memory forty years later.

I go on to say that for the past few days, I've been trying to get my head around what Dad meant. Because there is no way that he didn't mean it. Dad wasn't perfect, but he never lied to me. In business, his word was his bond. He was utterly without pretense.

No, he meant it. He believed it. If you heard it, he not only thought that you mattered — he delighted in you. I heard it around his office, in the way he had nicknames for everyone. The way he'd always put an arm around the little old lady receptionist. Even when he was razzing you, your presence, your life, was a joy to him. You were the greatest.

It's beginning to make sense to me, I say to the assembled crowd. I'm a new father. In holding my newborn son, I've begun to understand what Dad must have felt. The spontaneous joy, welling up from out of nowhere. The unsummoned happiness. The wild love.

But what I didn't know standing there that day, was how much I'd come to doubt his words. How hollow they'd sound. How meaningless.

"Remember, you're the greatest" — what once was a blessing would soon sound impossible and cruel.

THIRTEEN
THE LAST RIDE OF THE IMPALA

When I was fourteen, my father drove me through the gate of Assumption Cemetery and stopped the car.

"Okay, Johnny Appleseed, your turn," he said. And leaving the engine running, he got out and walked around to my side.

Off-lease from his company and battered by fellow salesmen, our Chevy Impalas were a fixture of the family. At one point, our driveway had three of them grazing. Unlike their namesake, the African antelope, they were neither light nor fleet of foot. No, Dad wanted to put mass on our side. He certainly didn't believe in seat belts. But put two tons of Detroit steel around a dreamy kid? He might have a chance.

I settled in behind the wheel and started off around the cemetery's loop. A thrill went through me; not only was I driving, but it had been Dad's idea. He trusted me.

Well, he trusted me to not kill dead people, anyway.

As we rounded one of the curves, I saw a funeral procession. Dad told me to slow down. I let my foot off the gas and carefully idled around the hearse, past fluttering flags and flowers, hands at ten and two o'clock.

Twenty-six years later, I drive through the gate of the cemetery and peer out the foggy windshield of Dad's huge car, trying to navigate my way to his gravesite. The headstones are bigger now and more numerous. And near the back is Dad's site, in a new row of plots bordered by a field of corn.

As we sing and pray and say goodbye, I rock Sammy in a zip-up blanket, trying to keep him warm.

I am forty, holding my son. My father had been forty when he first held me. I hadn't known Dad's father. And my son wouldn't know mine.

I look up and stare at the western horizon. Past the new cemetery fence I can see them, flecked in snow — the broken cornstalks where Dad and I had once taken to the air.

FOURTEEN
THE ANGEL IN THE OVERCOAT

After I helped my father resurrect the Ski-Doo in our garage that night, he drove us wild into the night toward the cemetery. It comes back to me vividly.

I am eight years old. All I can see in front of me is the back of my father. I cling to his waist, my arms around his overcoat, hanging on the back of the snowmobile. The freezing wind wicks moisture from my eyes, and the whine of the engine echoes off the walls of the mausoleum.

There's a rumble and crush as the Ski-Doo leaves the perimeter of the cemetery and jumps across the snow-covered furrows of corn like a skipping stone. I lean around Dad to try to see what's ahead of him. And within the vignette of darkness around the headlight's cast, I see his quarry, bounding away from us — the hindquarters of a whitetail deer.

We rise and fall over the swell of snowdrifts as the deer darts this way and that, trying to escape this strange predator.

Up ahead is a barbed wire fence and the deer makes for it, jumps, clears it, and Dad whips the Ski-Doo into a turn at the last minute. As the deer disappears into the darkness, we make for home.

I lay the side of my head against his back and keep my arms around his waist. Bare branches of a thousand oak trees pierce the deep blue of the horizon. The stars shimmer with the light of millennia past. It is dark and cold and holy beyond words.

The headlight of the snowmobile reflects off the snow, outlining the shape of my father in a halo of white light, an angel in an overcoat and black rubber boots.

We cut across the field, come to the edge of the cemetery and turn, following its boundary back home in a long slow arc, circling eternity.

PART TWO
LOST IN THE CANYONS

Nobody has ever measured, not even the poets, how much the heart can hold.

ZELDA FITZGERALD

ONE

SAFE

I've been sitting in the ER for four hours.

A doctor brings me a clipboard to sign. He explains that I'm waiving the hospital of liability for a CAT scan. He says that one X-ray is like a day in the sun, but a CAT scan is fifty. I think about how Sammy looks on the beach. How Lori slathers him in coatings of sunblock like spread cream cheese. The doctor mentions the words *cancer, kids,* and *radiation* far too close together in the same sentence.

I sign and follow the tech down the hall to radiology. Lori carries Sam, asleep in her arms. Somehow that makes it worse. He just appears more vulnerable.

We walk into a huge room with a high ceiling. In the center of it is a donut shaped circle, nine feet tall. Out of the donut hole is a platform where the tech lays down a radiology vest — the kind you get at the dentist — and Lori lays Sam on top of it. The tech puts another vest on top of Sam.

His bright blond hair peeks out from beneath. Red lines in the shape of a crosshair appear on Sam's forehead. The tech puts a vest on me. Silently, the platform moves toward the donut. Sam's binky moves up and down, in and out of his mouth, but he doesn't wake.

All the techs go into the control room where it's safe. And I'm behind my stupid vest where I'm safe. But that little head, where mysterious storms are blowing beneath that gentle brow — he's in there all alone.

IT WAS three days ago when it happened the first time. Sam, nine months old, was sitting in his booster chair and suddenly leaned over, his face twitching, his eyes glassy. When Lori described it to me that night, I thought she might have caught Sam with his making-a-diaper face.

But Lori knew her baby. This was different, she said. He seemed to look right through her like she wasn't there.

And then I see it the next day. His head jerks. And his face, his beautiful face, disappears behind a quivering mask.

All I've done for nine months is keep my little buddy safe. Strapping him into baby seats. Supporting him in shopping carts. Safe — you don't know much as a new dad, but you know that.

You support their head because they can't hold it up. Then you make sure they don't fall over when they sit down, because they will, and they do, but you catch them. You pull things out of their mouth, you rock them to sleep, you comfort them when they're crying. Safe. As a dad, you can't do much, but safe is your gig and you've got this.

Until you don't.

Now, something had snuck in behind my back. It's invisible. No gun, no deadbolt — nothing was going to stop this from breaking in. I was at my post. But it came anyway, and now my son shakes like he's possessed.

No one is safe. Safe is a sham.

TWO

UNKNOWN TERRAIN

The room with the big donut was two days ago. Or maybe it was three. I think today is Tuesday. Nights and mornings run together in a pastiche of cold hospital food, hard furniture, and the fluorescent glow over the sink near Sam's crib in pediatrics.

Now I stare at a different video monitor. This time, it's not a cardiogram for my father nor an ultrasound probing Lori's tummy. It's an EEG of my nine-month-old son. A scrolling set of a dozen lines bounces across the screen. A seismograph of my baby's broken brain.

A year ago, Sam's heartbeat from the womb — it had been straightforward. Pulsing with mystery, yes, but I knew it when I heard it.

This screen is keeping its own counsel. The machine is silent, but the picture is noisy. Filled with chaotic movement. And no one has told me what I am looking at, what each of these lines even mean. The part of the cortex where dreams originate? Autonomic control of digestion?

On the right half of the monitor, next to the scrolling jagged lines, is a closed circuit video of my son. In contrast to the movement of the EEG, Sam sleeps peacefully. But not for long. About once an hour, he has a seizure, and the lines bounce around like they're tracking a tremor.

Sam's head is swaddled in bandages in the shape of a minaret. Underneath those, are two dozen electrodes glued to his scalp, twisting into a summit of one electrical cord that snakes its way to the machine. I hold in my hand a red button at the end of a long cord, like a game show buzzer.

Since 11:00 a.m. yesterday, the EEG has been taking a continual readout of Sam's electrical brain activity. Every time he has a seizure, I press the red button to bookmark it. Tomorrow, the mapping lab will look for these digital markers, cross reference the video that's capturing Sammy's frozen limbs and disfigured face, and try to make sense of the whole damned thing.

There is also an adhesive patch on Sam's chest tracking his pulse. And like a year before when we heard it from the womb, his heart seems to be just fine. But mine is lost, wandering in a valley of jagged lines.

IN TIMES of trouble Dad would often say, "It's always darkest before the dawn."

The dawn hours — that's usually when Dad would call, once he retired. He would conveniently forget the two-hour difference between Chicago and the West Coast, and with time on his hands, ring me up. I would answer groggily, mumbling something about how advertising agencies get started around ten and so, no, I'm not up yet, Dad.

"You don't say!" Dad would exclaim, as if he was hearing that fact for the first time. Then again, Dad didn't quite understand what I was doing in digital advertising. I was in new tech, and he was already in old: Dad's first and only foray onto the Web was courtesy a giant Gateway PC, given by his company as a retirement gift in 1998. Dad had gotten an America Online account and he rarely, if ever, directed that bovine computer beyond the familiar confines of AOL and its faux browser. To be sure, Dad had never seen any of my ads. But he did forward to me, every day, a dozen articles about Y2K.

I wish I could ring him up now and get back at him with a wakeup call of his own. I just want to hear his voice ask the same questions about whether or not my car is running or if I need money.

I can't call Mom, lost as she is in the fog of Alzheimer's. Her short term memory is on a ten-minute loop. If I call, she will, within moments of hearing the news, ask how Sam is doing as if he isn't in the hospital.

But if Dad was on the phone with me now, sure as the world, he would sign off with his favorite goodbye, "Keep the faith," a phrase I'd heard him say a thousand times but still struggled to understand.

And he probably wouldn't be able to resist one more *bon mot*. Trying to be of comfort, he'd likely say before hanging up, "It's always darkest before the dawn, John Boy."

I HEAR something in Sam's crib, and go to press the red button for the hundredth time. False alarm. It's just Sammy moving around. He rolls over, blinks open his eyes, and goes back to sleep. As he puts his face against the pillow he says something in baby talk that I can't make out. I'm doing the same. My prayers ache, but I have run out of words.

That dark night, I had no idea how far afield Sam would lead us. How his descent into the valley of his condition would lead us into shadows I'd never traversed. As he had told me on those newborn nights when he wouldn't look into my eyes, this life would be on his terms. But I had no idea how much my terms, my very conception of things like justice and suffering, were going to be led down trails where shafts of light would struggle to get in.

I look out Sam's hospital window. Still dark. There's no sign of sunlight on the surrounding mountains. And the lines on the EEG keep rising and falling, drawing a schematic of an unknown terrain.

THREE
WONDER IN REVERSE

Early that morning, a neurologist comes into Sammy's room and introduces himself. Dr. C. has glasses and a white, trimmed goatee like Colonel Sanders. His black leather doctor's bag is right out of a Frank Capra movie.

He takes Sammy in his arms with genuine interest, not clinical but tender. He gently snaps his fingers in either of Sammy's ears. Sammy is cheery, oblivious to the mass of cords spilling out of his swaddled-up scalp.

Dr. C. patiently listens to us explain the last few days. He tells us that the CAT scan isn't uncovering anything, which is good; that it found no spots means there's no pathology. But it also means there's no explanation to the seizures.

Then we catch a break. Right in front of Dr. C., Sam has a seizure. The doctor stares intently from Sam to the EEG monitor and back to Sam again. His eye is trained on two of the lines which are now leaping around the screen more erratically. After about forty seconds, it ends.

An EEG specialist will be reviewing the video and the graphs and making a precise report. But Dr. C. has seen enough. He writes a prescription and tells us that we can leave the hospital today. The prescription is for an anticonvulsant to treat epilepsy.

Wait, epilepsy? I'd heard of it, but know little about it. A close friend had gotten it at eighteen, but had largely controlled it with medication for the past fifteen years. One of my favorite authors, Fyodor Dostoyevsky, had epilepsy.

Epilepsy, I learn, occurs when the neurons signal abnormally. Neurons typically generate an electrical current to produce actions, thoughts, emotions, and a million other things. But with epilepsy this current gets amped out of control, like lightning hitting a transformer. In a seizure, neurons fire wildly at up to 500 times a second, and this surge has to go somewhere, causing the involuntary movement that we've been witnessing for the past several days.

As he leaves, Dr. C. encourages us. He says most kids, about 70 percent, grow out of it.

A nurse comes by our hospital room to shampoo the adhesive out of Sam's hair. As the minaret is unspun revealing the electrodes glued to his scalp, Sam holds the railing of his crib and bounces around like a dog being checked out of a kennel.

But I am in a daze, awash in feelings I can't even articulate.

My mind drifts back to a night last summer, a few months before the seizures began. We were at The Americana in Glendale. The place is a bit too Disneyland for me. They have a trolley, and the old-timey façades of the stores are a bit too crisp and perfect.

But five-month-old Sam couldn't care less for my snobby architecture pique. He couldn't stop looking at everything.

Sam was in front of me facing forward. My arm was in a U-shape, my palm facing me, and he sat in the crux of my arm like a sailor straddling a mast. He was the king of the world swinging and gaping at the ocean of faces and light that came at him. He wasn't missing a thing.

We walked up to the fountain. Every half hour or so, it went off, skyrocketing jets of water in time to Rat Pack music. Twisting nozzles flung water in liquid pirouettes.

And I watched Sam, watching. His eyes followed the water into the air and back down. His head turned, following the twirling streams.

We left the fountain and walked into the Puma store. Sam just gazed, the electric tint of the shoes washing over him.

I found myself thankful. *How cool is this?* I thought. *I get to see a tiny person see something for the first time. I get to watch him experience awe.* His unsullied perception moved me.

Of course, not every night was like that walk around the fountain. There was newborn drudgery. But even in the midst of that very manual labor, he pointed us toward wonder. The most inconsequential thing, when noticed by Sam, became a sacred pause in the midst of my hurry.

Rain on the windowsill, the blur of a blue jay — for nine months, Sam had been delighted by every last thing, and so were we. He made us look through his eyes and see the world all over again.

But now, the world is being remade. I see Sam tremble in a seizure and I don't want the naive wonder of a child. I'd like everything explained right now, thank you very much.

For nine months, there had been no sign of any deficiencies. He was in the normal percentiles. He even showed some pluck and peed right at his doctor the moment before his circumcision. From day one, he'd been our happy appendage.

But that was healthy Sam. Sam with all his fingers and toes. Not Sam with his body convulsing, and his face contorted every hour. This wasn't how it was supposed to go. It was supposed to keep going the way it had been going: Sam, the welcome conqueror of our little condo. Spit-up, diapers, who cares? We were in love with our little man. Life was upside down, but like two sloths, we sleepily moved through inverted days. We were exhausted but happy.

Now I'm the one seeing something for the first time: every limb, every one of his joints, locks in place like it's welded. His mouth grimaces as his head snaps uncontrollably. And I couldn't care less about the beautiful iridescence of water in a fountain. Burn the lilies of the field. I want some answers.

I realize that I've always put wonder — the mysterious, the inexplicable — on the bright side of the ledger. Yes, suffering moved me. When some tornado ravaged a Midwest town, Lori and I picked up the phone and called World Vision just like everybody else. But bad things have been an abstraction that other people deal with.

Nothing feels abstract now. I live on a hair-trigger of dread.

Mystery has fractured into confusion.

And when I see Sam's face twisted in convulsions, it is wonder in reverse. It is horror.

FOUR
I WANT A NEW DRUG

A new seizure makes me jump like the crack of a gun. We're two weeks into this and I'm still not used to it.

And worse, Sam's convulsions are getting more frequent. We call Dr. C. and he tells the pharmacy to increase the dosage of the anticonvulsant. They fade, but come roaring back the next day. Another phone call. Dr. C. doubles down on the meds again and Sammy's body doesn't respond.

A week later, Dr. C. changes the meds hoping to break the demon's back. And the seizures just get worse. I'm working on the other side of Los Angeles when Lori calls and says to meet her in the ER right away. The convulsions are not only lasting longer, but unlike the previous ones, Sam cries in pain when he comes out of them.

I race across town, but I feel weird. Strangely normal. Have I already adjusted? Have I put my emotions on a shelf to be sorted later?

I get to the ER and Sam is dazed, not himself. Not in a seizure but something worse: he doesn't recognize me. His mascara-commercial eyelashes, his towhead hair — the pieces are there, but something is off.

Where's his humor? His funny imitative faces? Over the last few months, he'd gotten so good at making faces that we'd begun to name them — The Ingrid Bergman, The Winston Churchill. Where's that jovial smile? I want my son back, dammit.

Everything about this is wrong. My mom is having trouble recognizing people, too, but she's in her seventies with Alzheimer's. Ten-month-old babies don't do much, but they do recognize their parents.

Come back, Sam, come back to me.

A thought occurs to me and I can't send it back: what if the seizures are damaging Sam's personality, his development, his ability to be himself? My emotions jump off their place on that shelf like soup cans shaking to the floor in an earthquake.

And then Sam just comes out of it. He smiles and does his mug-for-the-camera head tilt. He's back. And for some reason, the seizures are gone. After an hour of quiet, the ER sends us home.

The next day Dr. C. apologizes. He should have told us to combine Sam's old prescription and the new one. We thought we were supposed to replace it. And that brought us to the ER.

I'm angry but I let it go. Dr. C. has been a saint. Has kept his cell phone on at all hours. Did he tell us, in our sleepless state, to combine the meds? Should the pharmacist have said something? Blame is pointless.

We combine both the anticonvulsants, but the seizures persist. Dr. C. says that you can keep trying new drugs — there are dozens — but with each successive treatment, the efficacy tapers off. Kids who are most likely to have their seizures controlled with anticonvulsants get traction on the first or second med they try. But with the third regimen, the likelihood of stopping seizures goes down to five percent or less.

Sam is not responding well. He's on his second med. He's slipping down the slope of that statistical chart.

Every morning, I shove this data to the back of my brain and go to work. I tell myself that Sam will be a kid who grows out of it. That the odds are on our side. We just have to give it some time. And when a seizure comes, I can be detached, almost clinical.

But then I catch a glimpse of his face, his unrecognizable face.

IT'S LATER on that winter. Sam is learning to walk in our grassy yard. He takes a step and then — wham — a seizure knocks his feet out from under him, a bully pushing him to the ground. I curse myself for not seeing it coming, pick him up in my arms, and tell him over and over that I'm here, wondering if he can hear me. Where is he, right now? What is his view from those oddly frozen eyelids? He comes to, but he's too young for words. Can't tell me how it feels. And then gets up and starts walking again. Sammy the Brave.

He toddles down the sidewalk, gripping each of my index fingers in his fists, like a Harley biker with handlebars above his head.

I put one foot in front of the other, walking behind him and giving him encouragement. But my fear for what's next stalks alongside.

FIVE
BREAKING DOWN THE STAGE

Stacks of drawers are on top of drawers. One of these towers is bound to crash. What will break down first, one of us, or that teetering pile we just pulled from inside the kitchen island?

I'm at Mom and Dad's house. He's been gone a year. We've all come into town to clean it out and get it ready for sale. But there's eighty years of stuff to sort through. And it's become clear that the Greatest Generation didn't just win a war, they were the greatest at keeping everything. Every. Last. Thing.

As she goes through the flotsam of one more overflowing cabinet, a soft groan of anger emanates from my sister, Sarah. She finds unredeemed pie tins from the local restaurant mixed in with the good pewter. Wha—? Has Dad laid some scavenger hunt from the grave?

Then I find something I've never seen before, a beat up folio with brass clasps. I pull open the dusty brown leather and inside is a tidy history of Bollow Better Built Homes, the little construction company Dad formed with his brother and his dad after World War II. I pull out a sheet of paper, tri-folded. It's a profit and loss statement for the three partners, plunked out on a typewriter by my grandfather. Together, they built about ten houses on the North Side of Chicago, including one on Kenton Avenue in Skokie, where I spent the first four years of my life.

The same house where my father, just like me, had left for the hospital in a fright, carrying his son in his arms.

DAD WOULD OFTEN TELL that story. When I was a toddler, I tripped over the telephone cord in their bedroom and hit my forehead on the glass top of a side table. When Dad found me, he couldn't believe all the blood. He pressed a washcloth to my forehead but still it came. Mom took my older brother and sister to the neighbors and they tore off to the hospital.

Dad would always begin that story the same way. He'd take my head in one hand, and with his other, gently pull back the hair from my forehead till he could see the edge of my scalp. He would stare at the top of my forehead and say, "He stitched you up pretty well." The faint outline of the scar is still there when I look in the mirror, like the fossil of an inchworm.

That evening in 1969 when he sped to the hospital with Mom holding ice cubes in a dishrag to my bleeding forehead: in that moment, what had he felt?

I'd like to know. Wish I could talk to him now. Because I cannot capture what I feel when I see Sam in a seizure. Helpless, terrified, emasculated? It is all those words and a hundred more feelings that have no name.

Did he say to me what I say to Sam when the right half of his little face goes so wrong, goes missing for a full minute? He's right here in my arms but a million miles away and I call him back from some far off place:

"You're okay, buddy, Daddy's here, you're okay."

Those emotions passed for my father. But for years to come, he'd take my face in his hands and tenderly pull back my bangs, parting the curtain on that memory one more time.

When I was a kid and Dad would do that, it felt a little odd because of course I had no memory of him tearing down Howard Street, blowing the stoplights in his Ford Galaxie 500, and roaring up to the ER at Evanston Hospital.

Like Dad, will I get to tell this story in the past tense? Will I take Sam's face in my hands looking in vain for some sign of distress and happily reassure myself of the outcome?

"Outcome" — will we ever get one of those? A real diagnosis and a real cure? Or will everything just go on and on like my mother's Alzheimer's?

I NEED SOME AIR. I carry a ladder to Dad's hidden bookcase.

While Dad had built our first two homes, he'd left this one to someone else. But it still had his touch. He'd asked the builder to turn the garage ninety degrees because he never liked garage doors to face the street. He'd built some cabinets for my mom's home business.

And upstairs, in the reaches of the vaulted ceiling off the master bedroom, Dad had designed a belfry of a bookshelf. You'd never know it was there and that might have been intentional; he could never stop lending books and then decrying their lack of return.

I look up from the narrow hallway that runs between their closets and see the treasure trove of history books. The top shelf nearly touches the twelve-foot ceiling. I climb the ladder and run my finger along the spines, dust jackets torn from all the times that I'd stuffed them into my knapsack to show off at school.

Back downstairs, Sarah finds a diamond in the dust. Not just a love letter, but a please-come-back letter. Dad's leaning cursive is the same as ever, but everything else is news — they'd broken up? At some point during their five-year courtship, Mom had shown him the door. Contrite words spill from his fountain pen. He says he's been wrong. He expresses her qualities. The letter is a stethoscope, revealing a heart we thought we knew.

On the kitchen counter is a traffic jam of old coffee mugs. I pick up one of his favorites, forever stained with his weak Hills Bros. coffee, a watery bilge I couldn't stand. But on the mug are painted three of our beloved planes, the Mustang, Spitfire, and Flying Fortress. To a thrift store it would be less than junk. But I pack it in one of my boxes like it's crystal. I find his flight log, his aviation headset and his airport maps, sole survivors of solo flights in that old Cessna.

I walk into their living room and come across Mom's porcelain bird collection. I see her miniature Christmas village, which Dad would set up for her every year. And her bone china with the gold-leaf edge, which was only brought out for holidays.

But I can't feel anything anymore, except the powdery dust darkening my hands. My brain is tired of separating the meaningful from the meaningless.

Everything just feels like a prop. The magic of the play is gone. The house lights are up, the sets are exposed. The grand thespian has made his exit. And his co-star is wandering the stage they shared, her memories fading day by day.

I finish placing Dad's aviation books in the last of my boxes, and the packing tape goes on with a screech and a tear.

SIX

HOW TO COMPARTMENTALIZE A SOUL

It's time for another test, this time an MRI, "magnetic resonance imaging." Nothing is resonating in me. I am numb.

Hadn't we just done this last year? Gotten all three of us ready for the hospital?

It had felt so different then. Sam was about to be born. We went loaded with excitement. Packed the electrolytes for Lori and the cheat sheet for me.

As we drive to the hospital, I try to tell myself that others have it worse. Recently, a woman Lori knows had a baby with half a heart who's clinging to life. His parents have lived at the hospital for months. I think about the kids we see at the neurologist's office who are strapped to a recumbent wheelchair, kids whose limbs and faces remind me of Sam at his worst moments. Kids who never snap out of it.

Comparisons loop in my brain. I keep telling myself, "Well, that's not us anyway." And it makes me feel better. For a minute. And then I'm back to what our life has become: catching Sam when he has a seizure, telling Sam he's okay when he comes out of it, and talking with doctors who have no answers. I don't live someone else's story, I live ours. But no one can tell me how this story will end, or even how to get to an ending. We're told to try drugs and hope. That's it?

In the MRI prep room, the anesthesiologist hands me another clipboard and recites the risks of putting Sam under. He says that Sam is in more danger when riding in a car on the freeway than he is from anesthesia. I scan the pages, but why bother? All the legal gobbledygook just reminds me of how powerless I've been. I sign robotically.

Like every day, I hold down the dread, try to be there for Sam, and compartmentalize to function. But inside me, there's not much room left. The storage unit is full and I can't get the door closed. Because I'm running out of places inside myself to tuck away all this garbage, all these drugs that don't work, and one more test that will probably come back with, "Nothing to see here, folks."

I keep trying to tell myself that Sam's life can't be judged by its defects, but by its opportunities. Weak clichés loop through my head. I sound like a pathetic stanza from a greeting card.

Two of the pastors from Sam's Sunday School, Viv and Carlos, show up to be with us outside of the MRI lab. How did they even know we were here? As they pray, partitions inside me implode like a collapsing building. I sag into Carlos's arms, weeping. A song I learned in Sunday School when I was just a little guy runs through my mind:

> Red and yellow, black and white,
> they are precious in his sight,
> Jesus loves the little children of the world.

I think of those words. But God's love is not safe. Trusting God is not wish fulfillment. To paraphrase old Job, *Who knows what He will do?* You hear all the time about parents with broken kids, kids who die, and then those parents find out that someone heard their story and was touched and changed and isn't that special.

And as Sam goes under I silently plead: *Please don't make us be that special story. I don't want to be that special story.*

JUST LIKE THE CAT-SCAN, the MRI comes back normal. Sure, it's good that there's no tumor or anything else. But it moves us further into the generic yet all too common description of Sam's epilepsy: "unexplained seizures."

With no prognosis, Sam's life stretches out before me as neither terminal nor healed. Only a hope of controlling the seizures until he grows out of them.

If he grows out of them.

SEVEN
GRAND CANYONS

I stand on the edge of the North Rim and stare into the rippling rock. Miles of mist filter the bands of color into lavender and pale magenta. It's Memorial Day and we've taken Sam for his first camping trip to the Grand Canyon.

His little hiking shoes are scuffed at the toes; he's sixteen months old and walking. Six months into the epilepsy. He clambers over some rocks that look like a jumble of coffee tables. He grips the next shelf of stone, raises one knee to get a bit more elevation, then stands triumphantly, grinning from beneath his outdoorsy sunhat.

Dad loved the Grand Canyon. So much so that he drove all the way around so we could see it from both sides. The South Rim has more spectacular views but gets twenty-five times the visitors. In contrast, the North Rim remains a quiet eyrie, with just a few lookouts and a scattering of cabins huddled around the old stone lodge.

I was seventeen when Dad rented two burros so he and I could descend into the depths. Of course, my frugal father didn't want to spring for the whole burrito. I had wanted us to ride all the way to Phantom Ranch on the shores of the Colorado, but Dad balked at the price. So we only went halfway down into the orange shades of strata, Dad's body swaying in the saddle, left then right like a metronome set on slow. That was our last family vacation together.

I stare across the canyon at the South Rim. I can see the tiny etching of Bright Angel Trail with its switchbacks going to the bottom. But my own path feels like a dead end. All the majesty can't shake my dread of what's waiting back at home.

As Sam's neurons have gone haywire, other parts of my life have blown out. We sold our condo as the market crashed and it put a hit on our savings. The recession has caved the advertising industry and my consulting work has mostly withered. The one new client I landed is refusing to pay my final invoice. And Sam's mounting medical bills have whittled our checkbook down to its last thousand bucks.

Throughout his career, Dad had carved his own trail. Why can't I do the same? He had plenty of false starts after getting out of the Army in 1948. He tried television repair. Built houses. And like me, took about ten years to find a career that gave him the independence he craved and the relationships he adored.

But I can't stop feeling shame. Dad always worked, always got it done. We never went without. What if I fail my wife and child?

Dad was always compassionate to out-of-work buddies. There was Frankie, his lifelong friend, an entrepreneur who'd gone to prison on some tax charge. I remember Dad pouring him a cup of coffee and talking at our kitchen table for hours. Dad's friend, Tom, was another struggling soul who often came to Dad for counsel.

Dad loved his friends. Often found work for them. But I'd never known him to be on the other side of someone's kitchen table, never known him to be on the precipice we're on now.

I look out. The horizon reaches toward the sunset in long steps of foggy blue. The wind comes up the walls, tosses my wife's beautiful brown hair, and exhales through the pines. But I can't breathe deep, can't relax.

IT'S our last night on the North Rim. We pack our gear and grab one of the cabins so we can have a hot shower before hitting the road tomorrow.

Lying awake in bed, I can hear the wind outside. But the howling in my head won't quit. I'm a month away from not being able to pay our medical insurance. The drugs aren't working. And neither am I. I toss and turn and finally give up.

I step out of the cabin. The cold, 8,000-foot air goes through my jacket. Overhead, stars jewel the deep blue like they did when Dad and I would take snowmobile rides.

But I'm not the man my father was. Unlike Dad, the ace salesman, I can't catch this deer, can't even put it in my sights. I can't throttle up, can't cover the distance. How the hell did he pull everything off?

I know what you said, Dad, but I'm not the greatest, not at this.

I walk through the parking lot and get into our car.

I sit down, start the engine, and just scream. I hit the steering wheel over and over and yell at God. I tell him that I don't want this trail anymore. The canyon is too dark. The walls are too sheer. I don't have a map.

I shout into the darkness till I'm hoarse. I walk back to the cabin and like a baby exhausted from crying, drop into restless sleep.

The next day, we drive back to Pasadena — and down into one more black canyon. The insurance has authorized a second opinion at UCLA. For the past six months Dr. C. has been great, but it's time to see what someone else would say.

We're at UCLA's pediatric neurology. The resident physician comes in and, as casual as a waiter reciting salad dressings, says, "So, you're here for a brain surgery consult?"

We look at him dumbstruck. That's his opening? Cutting open my toddler's skull? We've been told for over six months that there's a decent chance that Sam will grow out of this, but why not a little brain surgery while we're waiting?

Hey, I'm forty-one with high cholesterol, let's talk about some heart surgery for me, too. Does that come with the salad?

I slowly recover. "No, this appointment was just for a second opinion. We didn't think we'd be talking about that." He looks at his clipboard and says that the appointment is to talk about brain surgery.

And one more time, a canyon opens up at my feet. Lori and I are both spooked. A few steps of a huge decision has just been leapfrogged with no warning. We leave UCLA without finishing the conversation.

Then we're off to see another doctor but this time it's not a neurologist. It's Lori's OB. We're pregnant again.

Soon, another heartbeat from the womb will presage a life to come. And this one will be different, right?

EIGHT
ARMCHAIR PHILOSOPHERS

Sam is having a seizure in the dried fruits and nuts aisle of Trader Joe's. I catch him as he tumbles and gently lower myself to the floor with him in my arms.

As he writhes, I stroke his hair and speak gently. "You're okay, Sammy, I'm here."

A fifty-something woman bends over us.

"Would you like me to call 9-1-1?" No, I reply, he's fine, this happens every day.

She doesn't walk away.

"He has epilepsy," I say, hoping that she will move on and find that rare cheese she came for.

It doesn't matter where we are, every stranger has an opinion.

"Epilepsy?" they say. "Oh, I hear kids grow out of that."

I stare back, my mind swirling with things I'd like to say: *Did you drop out of medical school due to your abysmal GPA? Or were you expelled for being an emotional menace?*

Instead, I'm far too kind.

"He might grow out of it, he might not," I respond tersely.

I hate explaining things because there's no explanation. So I shorthand everything. I don't want to talk about it.

But others do. Random strangers channel their inner Jonas Salk. And they've all read just enough on Wikipedia to share their thoughts on neurology. Onlookers, acquaintances, whoever, just say whatever will make them feel better.

They'll say, "He seems better today!"

Why? Because he's not seizing in front of you this very minute?

Sam's condition is doing something inside them. He's rehabbing their beliefs about life. And in response, they try to spackle their cracking paradigm of a benevolent universe. They look for ways to make it better than it is.

I wish they'd realize for one second that it's not Sam that needs fixing. It's their unexamined assumptions.

I'm certainly looking at mine. For example, these words of Isaiah have always moved me with an intimate picture of God:

> *Even these may forget, but I will not forget you.*
> *Behold, I have inscribed you on the palms of My hands....* [4]

But I don't know what those words mean anymore. Has the Unforgetting One forgotten Sam?

I've always believed that each person is designed by God with intent and therefore has incalculable worth. But where in this calculus is Sam, or any child in any developing country who goes hungry and dies due to the accident of their birth?

"Accident." Is that what this is?

No, I can't believe that. I believe that each person is known from the womb. I've reveled in those words of Gerard Manley Hopkins, that the "Holy Ghost over the bent world broods, with warm breast and with ah! bright wings." I believe God superintends each cell that divides.

But how do I square that circle now? I don't believe that God has fled the scene, but He sure seems to be hiding. Olly olly in come free.

Because the explanations I'm getting from wannabe theologians aren't cutting it. Platitudes spill forth, this new wine bursting rotted wineskins.

ONE DAY I'm at a client's office and a conversation with a co-worker turns to our children and inevitably, to Sam.

"Everything happens for a reason," the person says about Sam. Ah, that old chestnut. I stare at my co-worker, my smile tightening. I don't know what to say. And what I want to say always occurs to me hours later:

Well, let's unpack that, Plato, since obviously you haven't bothered. "Everything happens for a reason." By "reason" you're implying a "justification," right? Well, then, play a little game with me, won't you?

Why don't you pick out the biggest, best "reason" you can imagine. Pick anything, any justification, okay? I'll give you a minute.

Got it? Good. And now I'll ask you a question: is your "reason" worth my son's suffering?

It is the rare person who simply says, "I'm so sorry," and just listens without offering advice.

Because Sam and his epilepsy are serving notice. His unjust suffering is dynamite in a mineshaft and no one likes a cave-in. It's difficult to breathe. You don't know if you're going to get out alive.

I know how they feel.

NINE
AND HE SHALL BE CALLED, HAWKWIND

Can everyone just shut up and mind their own business?

Anything involving a young child invites strangers to not only soapbox but intervene.

One night when Sam was a newborn, we'd adventurously met two friends for a double date at a Japanese restaurant. And like any baby new to earth, Sam was crying.

I walked around the restaurant trying to soothe him when a woman marched up to me, arms outstretched. "Give him to me," she demanded.

She didn't even introduce herself. I stared back at her. I had no idea what to say. Her face was oddly matter-of-fact, as if to say: *let me take care of this, rookie.* I half-turned away, shielding Sam. Her arms beckoned.

"No," I finally got out, "he's new."

And it's not just babies that cause this odd state of entitlement. Just walking around pregnant gives total strangers permission to chat up my wife.

We're at Target shopping. Lori is a few months away from her due date for Sam's new baby brother.

"What are you having?" comes the inquiry from a fellow shopper.

What are we having?

Madame, we are having a mammal. It will be warm-blooded and suckle. It will have vertebrae and opposable thumbs. It will not grow wings, or breathe through gills, though at some point in the future I'm sure trans-species surgery will make these things possible.

Can everyone just leave my introverted wife alone? Between having a child with epilepsy and her new pregnancy, Lori hasn't had to talk this much since she was a waitress.

The uninitiated conversation continues: "Have you picked out a name?"

Ah, baby naming. The unspoken game of one-upmanship. We've all gone overboard with baby names. And out here in Los Angeles, we've gone a bit cuckoo. Around here, any name that you've already heard of is deemed bourgeois. Instead, So-Cal moms and dads create their own names from scratch. They believe their child will one day be proud to go by the name of *Hawkwind* or *Winky*.

These parents are narcissists. I know. Because I have become one of those parents. I don't want just any old name. I tell myself that this pursuit is about making my kid's life more interesting, but it's not. It's about making me more interesting.

The problem is spreading. I read an article in the *Wall Street Journal* about baby-naming consultants. For several hundred dollars, this person will advise you on the rhythmic cadence of the syllables, write a full etymological background, and warn you if the name is too popular.

Thankfully, I married a sensible woman who can do her own demographic density analysis on the fly. Lori comes home from shopping one day and says, "I don't want to name the baby Aidan."

Lori had been at Target and in the space of about a half-hour, two different moms had called after two different little tykes, "Come here, Aidan, here Aidan." Two different families, two different kids, one Target — that's enough for Lori. She did not want our boy to be one of fifty at his school.

Aidan had been on her shortlist because her forebears came from the Emerald Isle. So we go looking for some Irish alternatives. We find a website where Frank McCourt pronounces each Irish name aloud and reads a short paragraph on its background. And let me tell you, when McCourt gets a hold of it, even *Kevin* sounds as smooth as eighteen-year-old whiskey.

Lori listens for a while and then decides she's done with all this falderal. If the man who wrote *Angela's Ashes* can't find her an Irish name, why bother? She leaves me to it.

But the blarney is only beginning. I find a site that offers up Welsh names. Let's hear it for *Teggwedd*! That's a lot of consonants. His grandparents would probably just call him "Ted."

I then direct my cursor to baby-naming websites that employ a random name generator. I spin that wheel of fortune. *Chul-moo* is the first name that comes up. It means "iron weapon."

I catch up with Lori. "Now, don't judge it until you've thought about it," I say, pausing for dramatic effect. "Iron Bollow!"

You will not run into any kid, at any Target ever, with that name. He could be a football player. If he goes into acting, he already has a stage name. And we've set him up to be the coolest contractor on the job site.

Lori is nonplussed by my sales pitch.

I confer some more with the bots, who promptly deliver up the following:

- Pasha – *"Passover" in Greek*
- Kahanu – *"the breath" in Hawaiian*
- Prem – *"affectionate love" in Sanskrit*

Nice meanings. But I give up on the online name-generator when I can't pronounce *Bugoneguig*, which means "hole in the sky" in a certain Native American tongue. Which is an excellent answer to the question: "Where do babies come from?"

I turn to another site whose algorithm produces a first and middle name pairing based on your surname. I type in my last name.

The result? *Deacon Christian Bollow*. Good heavens. No, actually, *Good Heavens Bollow* would be his sister, the Prohibitionist. Another website suggests *Bilhah*, one of Jacob's concubines.

So, biblically, we've covered the waterfront. But I'm not getting too far. And the more time I spend on this jag, the odder it becomes. I am speaking, of course, of the dreaded "We're Spelling It Differently" names.

Take for instance, *Dylan*. Nice name. I like Bob Dylan. Dylan Thomas has some great poetry. But according to the Social Security website, *Dylan* has consistently been in the Top 40, if you will. It's one of the most popular baby names of the previous few years. Like *Aidan*, you might run into one at Target. Oh, the gentrified shame of it all.

Therefore, hip parent, why not just change the vowel? *Dylon* is so interesting. That one vowel shoves it down to 980th in the Social Security new baby name rankings. And forces your child into a lifetime of correcting others' spelling: "No, it's D-Y-L-O-N, like nylon," he says for twenty years, until from exhaustion he changes his name to Dave.

Then *Ulises* comes up on my screen. Will you look at that? They've dropped the Y. People, you're already naming your kid after an epic poem. If you really want to stump grandpa at the spelling bee, just go with *Charybdis*.

IT'S the night of January 27, just two days after Sam's second birthday. Lori says she's not getting contractions so much as cramps. I remember that Sam's birthing marathon had run about thirty hours so I suggest to Lori that she go back to bed.

An hour later she's crouched over the white penny tile in our bathroom.

I'm on it! I pull out my iPhone and hit the stopwatch; I'm going to record those 4-1-1 contraction intervals. But they don't reveal a pattern. I tell Lori that I think she's still too early. If there's anything I remember from class, it's to not go to the hospital too soon. And if there's anything I've forgotten, it's that I don't really know anything.

Lori overrules me. This one is different, she says. She insists on leaving now. And, by the time we roll up to Arcadia Methodist, she is already at seven centimeters. This boy wants to get born in a hurry. Two hours later, all ten pounds and eleven ounces of man-child appears.

"Well, you won't be calling him *Tiny*," says the ever-understated Dr. G.

We name him Finley, "fair-haired warrior." And as we had done with Sam, we give our big boy a middle name that honors someone in the family, Stewart, the maiden name of Lori's great-grandmother.

And so the saga to name our second child landed on something Gaelic with a Scottish chaser, like my favorite whiskey.

But we may not have seen the end of it. Years later, Finley was brushing his teeth and looking into the mirror reflectively.

"I wish my name was Rocket," he said. "That's a name I could get used to."

TEN

THE HOMING BEACON

Sam has had epilepsy for eighteen months now. Seizures slice through our days like a bullwhip.

He's on his third anticonvulsant, but Sam won't be the poster child for this pharma company either. It not only doesn't stop the seizures, it makes him irritable and woozy. He drools out the bottom of his mouth, constantly dampening the front collar of his shirts. His two-year-old chin has a perpetual rash from all the saliva.

Then we get a call from another hospital in Los Angeles. A waiting list I got us on several months back finally has an opening with a well-known specialist. We drive over.

She is perfunctory and chilly. Seems like she's in a rush. She glances through Sam's records and says he'll never grow out of it. After twenty minutes, she gets up to go and says we should try more of the third drug — the one that's made Sam grouchy and drooling. So she didn't get a good Yelp review. And we're back to Dr. C.

He prescribes a fourth anticonvulsant. Nothing changes —

different cocktail, same seizures. As expected, the effectiveness of the drugs has dropped off a statistical cliff. It's coming up on the second anniversary of Sam's diagnosis and we've driven down another cul-de-sac. Is there any way out?

A year ago, talking about brain surgery seemed extreme, but now we're ready. We go back to UCLA to talk with a renowned surgeon. He looks over Sam's clipboard, annoyed. I feel like a kid sitting in the principal's office.

"You've been here before," he scolds. He chastises us for leaving a year ago, when we were spooked. For being too slow to explore surgery. He shares more statistics: that if we don't get Sam's epilepsy under control he could fall behind his peers and stay there for life. We agree to take the next step and schedule a battery of pre-surgical tests.

A FEW WEEKS before Sam's third birthday, we head back to UCLA for a three-day stay. Once again there's an EEG and Sam's head is wrapped up in the shape of a Russian steeple. There's a PET scan. More hard furniture. And the same hard news. On our last day there, the chief of pediatric neurology shares the test results. Sam is not a good surgical candidate. His electrical activity is not coming from a single address in the brain but from all over the zip code. And you don't cut away brain tissue unless you're sure of the seizures' exact origin.

We check out, Lori's stepdad carrying Sam. We walk behind, pulling a roller bag of dirty clothes down the airy, marble hallway endowed by Mattel Toys.

We walk through the warm brown paneling of the expansive waiting room filled with a dozen families. Fussy siblings are playing on iPads and underneath the furniture. A father in a trade union T-shirt sits motionless, elbows on knees, staring at his big hands knotted in front of him. But almost every mother is on her cell phone, updating the nerve endings of their wider families. We walk by a mom talking quietly, punctuating the call with bullet points she got from the doctor. Not many floors away, a child in an operating room is adrift in anesthesia, a little boat on a dark sea. But she will keep the bulletins coming, she will send the S.O.S. She will keep it together when everyone else is coming apart. Today, like every day, her needs are put aside. She will cry later, by herself, alone.

I'M BACK HOME NOW, in the dark of their bedroom. Finley sleeps next to Sam, flying to bright planets in his spaceship pajamas. But the landscape of Sam's dreams is broken by thunderbolts. He is seizing.

I kneel down and stroke his head as it quivers and jerks. I quietly say that he's going to be okay. But I don't know if I believe that anymore. I twist my fists into his bedspread and bury my face there.

In a whisper wet with tears I plead, "Make it stop. Please, heal him. Why don't you do something?"

I cannot account for what came next, but in my mind I hear a still small voice:

Don't you understand? He will be great.

Sam gets past the worst of the seizure, the pneumatic hammers in his body finally running out of steam. And in the silence, those quiet words pulse inside me, over and over:

Don't you understand? He will be great.

But my own question pounds back: "How? How can someone so broken ever be great?"

From the time he was a baby, I'd spoken my father's words over Sam, the same nine words that Dad had said to me: *Remember, as you go through life, you're the greatest.*

I'd said it, but did I believe it? Greatness, here? That specialist, she said Sam would never grow out of it. The brain surgeon at UCLA said that Sam could be behind for life.

Don't you understand? He will be great.

Kneeling over Sam's bed in the stillness, those two phrases keep repeating in a quiet persistence like the soft tone of the homing beacon in Dad's old Cessna. Dad had explained it to me thirty years ago as we were bumping along through the sky one day. It was the VOR, a radio beam in Morse code sent from small airports that helped him navigate his cross-country flights.

"As long as I hear that, John," Dad said, tapping the plane's dashboard, "we'll be fine. To stay on course, all I have to do is keep listening for that tone." When nothing below him looked familiar, he just kept listening for the beacon.

Don't you understand? He will be great.

I'm listening, Dad, but I don't understand. How will he ever be great?

PART THREE
THE ROCKS CRY OUT

And though my hard heart scarce to Thee can groan,
Remember that Thou once did write in stone.

ONE
DAD, YOU PRAY GOD

I walk in past our peeling blue paint to find a polliwog skimming across my path.

It is Finley — as in birth, so in life. He was just a few ounces shy of eleven pounds when he came barreling into our lives last year. And now he scoots down the hall with a speed that belies his mass. He is not yet walking, but I believe he has found a mode of transport that's faster.

He folds his chubby left leg beneath his body, reaches forward, big hands slapping then pulling at the hardwood floor, and pushes himself from behind with his right leg.

Front arms flailing like a game of leapfrog, back half like a tadpole, he is a landbound amphibian, a Darwinian cheat of physics and friction.

And he knows that he delights. He looks up at me through sandy bangs, past freckles sprinkled on cupcake cheeks. He holds my glance for a moment with those hazel eyes of my father's and then sets off again, swimming down the hallway floor.

Sam, looking on, is far less sure of his motions. He steadies himself against the plaster wall made grubby by his toddler brother.

He's learned the hard way to always be ready for a seizure; walls and tables are often touched as he walks. And upon sensing a seizure coming on, he'll run towards the big green chair in the living room. He doesn't always make it.

He looks up at me in earnest.

"Dad, you pray, you pray God," he says, staring at me. "You pray God, 'No more seizures.'"

I kneel down, hug him, and say that I'll pray. But I don't know what good it's going to do. It had been done a thousand times over, all over the country. Friends back home and nearby. All his little cousins at bedtime, his grandparents worried sick — who hasn't prayed for my son?

One of my friends who had been out of work for several years had told me recently how it felt: "I feel like my prayers are a letter to God that's fallen behind his desk."

We are still on a waiting list for a new experimental program. Sam's seizures ripple through his body, up to thirty a day. And Sam's anticonvulsants have a mind of their own. Some days they work. But on bad days they're just soaked sandbags against a flooding river, as the epilepsy courses through his body like a thunderstorm.

But in his fog, my three-year-old son grasped at some invisible shaft of light. Something in his mind burned brighter than the next aura and he said to me with a faith greater than mine:

"Dad, you pray, you pray God. You pray God, 'No more seizures.'"

TWO
FORCE-FEEDING A CURE

I wake in the middle of the night to the acrid smell of vomit.

I look over at Sam's hospital bed, and already, silent saints are moving in and out of the shadows of his half-lit room.

I can't understand their equanimity as they pull off one more wet pillowcase, strip the sheets, and mop the floor.

I shuffle over as they gently remove Sam's dirty hospital gown. I take him into my arms. Exhausted, he lays his towhead on my shoulder. He's about to turn four and most of his life has been a war.

I thank them. I apologize. I feel like I should be the one cleaning up.

They just smile, lay out a fresh garment, and say that's why they're here.

The little clown pattern on the fresh hospital gown mocks the whole scene. Nothing is funny about this. Since he was admitted the day before, Sam has vomited ten times.

We've been told that's normal, but I don't know what normal

means anymore. This is a road unlike any other part of Sam's journey. After a year on a waiting list, Sam has been admitted to the ketogenic program at UCLA, a therapy that will radically transition his daily diet to fat in hopes of arresting the seizures. While randomized controlled studies have shown that it reduces seizures in over half of those who try it, and some claim that 25 percent are cured, the scientific reason why "keto" is working on so many children at UCLA is a mystery.

But what is already clear is what we were warned about. Sam's body has to adapt to breaking down food in a whole new way. His body chemistry has to change how it gets energy. It has to be retrained from the way all of us get fuel, from glucose, and has to be forced into "ketosis," a condition where energy will be taken from fat. From now on, 75 percent of his diet will be made up of fat.

And his body isn't liking it. Fat doesn't break down as easily in the digestive system. A switch has to be flipped in Sam's metabolism and as it fights its natural course, nausea is the only change we're seeing.

As the orderly finishes changing Sam's bedsheets, I sit down on the vinyl pullout. I've been sleeping on its concrete softness in snatches. Lori is at home, seven-months pregnant with our other news, a third baby boy. In the morning she will drive back with an insulated picnic bag filled with her new homework, exacting recipes of fat-laden concoctions.

A nurse comes in and says that Sam is dehydrated and needs an IV. Sam wakes and cries as he's pricked and I tell him he's brave. She leaves and he pulls at the bandage where the IV has gone in.

"Sammy the Brave," I say, and gently bring his hand away from the IV. "Sammy the Brave," I repeat until he falls asleep and I lay him back on the fresh sheets. I stumble over to the pull-out and open my laptop. My two clients have been understanding about me working remotely, but there's emails to return, invoices to send. So the glow of my Macbook, and the light near Sam's crib, burn into the night.

THE EXPECTED four to five day stay has become a week. Sam's body fights the metabolic shift. Lori goes back and forth to our home, stands on aching pregnant feet, trying to teach herself this oily art. Packs everything in a cooler and drives thirty miles through traffic every morning. Gets here, gives Sam his first keto-meal — only to have him throw up all her hard work.

And if Sam has just taken his meds, the vomit can't be discarded. Sam still needs his anticonvulsants to complement the diet. So we carefully look through every discharge for the telltale capsule.

It's Groundhog Day. Sammy slowly eats, tries to keep it down, and sometimes can't. Sammy gets his blood drawn and cries. Sam asks about the whereabouts of his toddler brother and asks all day to watch the movie, "Cars." In the background, Owen Wilson's earnest voice adds a manic soundtrack to this scene we can't escape.

One morning, Sam wakes earlier than usual and the stopwatch starts in my brain. To stay on track, he needs to get his keto breakfast inside of him.

Lori texts me to say she's leaving as soon as she can. Measuring everything on the scale, the exhaustion of pregnancy, Sam's bleary-eyed confusion — it's pulling her under.

Ten minutes later, she's on the side of the road, convulsed and crying, trying to explain to the cop why she was racing to the hospital. He's merciless. Writes the ticket. And Lori sheds ten miles of tears down the freeway. She's done. Let her boy come home.

I'm married to the strongest woman in the world. She's already staring down her last trimester. Mentally arranging how to add a third boy to our home. But Lori doesn't know where that will be; we want to buy our old Spanish house, but our landlord has not yet shown his cards.

We live between frayed edges, feeling for Sam in his trauma but not wanting to give up. A week at UCLA turns to ten days. The vomiting subsides. Sam's body may be adjusting but I'm not. Every time he stirs, I snap to attention, and grab a bedpan. Mindless plodding replaces hope. I'm too tired to hope. I just want relief.

Lori calls it. She tells the doctors we've had enough. Tells them that we'll keep going, but we'll keep going at home. They've been thinking the same thing; it's been eleven days. We get discharged.

But at home it gets worse. Sam has ten long, bad seizures, of a greater severity than we've ever seen. Another thirty that night. The earth slips off its axis, morning and night blur; has everything he's been through been for nothing?

Then, inexplicably, the seizures abate for a couple of days. It's mental whiplash.

The only thing that's clear is the electronic rectitude of Lori's new kitchen scale and its merciless accounting of every fraction of a gram.

Every recipe has to be looked up, made from scratch, and then logged online under the supervision of a dietician. From here on out, Sam cannot eat any of our food, he has to eat every four hours, and has to eat every glistening crumb within forty-five minutes.

Sam has always been a slow eater.

Lori throws another batch into the garbage; the scale says that she put in too much heavy whipping cream. I cover our couch in beach towels, surround the perimeter with mixing bowls to catch Sam's next bout of nausea, and slip Lightning McQueen into the DVD player.

"Ma-Queen," Sam says, staring at the screen, listless.

We reach our first Saturday back home. I take Sam and Finley to a park. I have to tell Sam that he can't have Finley's snack, despite his pleadings. When this madness started, I couldn't keep him safe. Now I can't keep him from feeling hungry.

This cure is custom-made to pummel the pride of fatherhood right out of me.

THREE

PLAGUE

The week after our release from the hospital, we have a low-key fourth and second birthday for Sam and Finley at Travel Town in nearby Griffith Park. We are surrounded by century-old steam engines as tall as our house. Finley looks up, jubilant, but Sam is groggy. Lori has prepared a substitute cake for him since things like frosting are now off limits. Sam, still in his weakened state, utters a weak "choo-choo," gazing glassy-eyed at the trains.

The next day, Lori wakes to an itchy feeling on the back of her head. In the bathroom, she scratches at her scalp and brings her hand around to look: there's a tiny louse in her fingernail. She stares at it.

"I cannot. Have a baby. While I have lice," she says, unbelieving. She checks the boys. Sam and Finley have it, too.

Couldn't you have sent one of the other plagues, God? Maybe turned the Los Angeles River to blood? Given that misbegotten concrete canal some character?

Life is triage. Lori tries to rid the boys of the pestilence. We add an anti-nausea drug to Sammy the Brave, but he keeps vomiting several times a week.

In addled desperation, Lori takes Sam and Finley to Supercuts to get their heads shaved. The horrified manager throws them out before they even get seated. So Lori sits them both down in the backyard, shaves their heads as smooth as billiard balls, marches their naked bodies into the bathroom, and scrubs them down with a soap that, I believe, was developed in the wake of Three Mile Island. Lori contemplates doing a full Sinéad O'Connor on herself but opts for a gooey toxin that she runs through her hair with a fine tooth comb.

We reach the final week of pregnancy. Go to the OB for one last visit.

If we heard a heartbeat or saw a gently floating shape, knees tucked under his chin, I have no memory of it.

And the day before he was born — did I pack some of Lori's favorite music to play in Labor and Delivery? Copy and paste that old cheat sheet to my iPhone?

All I remember is holding my day-old son and hearing the news that one of my dearest friends, Jack, was in a different hospital dying of pneumonia. On my phone, spliced between texts of congratulations, were dark words: *Get here as soon as you can.*

Jack? The marathon runner who had run with the bulls in Pamplona? No, not Jack, the kindest of all men. Don't take Jack, the selfless, the pure.

I drive across town, from our hospital to his. In the waiting room I hug old friends. We stare silently with eyes that all say the same thing: how can this be happening to someone so hale and hearty? He's only sixty-two.

While Jack was a lifelong bachelor, he had many "kids" as he called them. He was a mentor to hundreds in Hollywood, but never saw his name in lights. He didn't care. He gloried in others' successes. When we were roommates, I remember him pausing the DVR to check the credits before a show, gazing in pride at the names of his protégés.

It's my turn to be in his room. I take hold of his hand but he's unresponsive. The oxygen mask covers his face like some mockery of his days at the Air Force Academy where he trained to be a pilot like his father before him. But his gentle eyes are closed. He is swiftly flying away from me.

From all over the world come prayers for Jack, pleading all over his Facebook page. Please save this knight of a man. Heal this one we love.

He hangs on for two days, lungs laboring, and he's gone.

Senseless scenes collide. I hold my newborn and write a eulogy for Jack. Easter comes and Jack lies in a grave.

Some weeks later, I'm giving Finley and Sammy an evening bath. I turn to get Finley's teddy-bear towel off the hook, crouch down to get him out, and he says, "Do the bear, do the bear!"

Finley wants to see my funny dance. A while back, I'd started this nighttime routine where I'd take his towel — which has a teddy-bear sewn into the hood — pull it over my head, and clumsily dance, making bearish grunts.

I exit stage left to put on my costume. I go around the corner, put the bear's head over my head — and just stop. I can't take another step. Can't summon the joy. Out of view of the boys, I start crying.

Finley calls for me. But there's no cash in my emotional drawer. I slide to the floor, pull the towel over my face and sob.

After a few minutes, I collect myself, scoop them up out of the tub, and carry them to their bedroom. I pull some jammies out of the closet and set Sammy in front of me. He knows something's wrong; Daddy didn't do the bear. As I'm drying him off, Sammy stares at me and says, "Sorry, Daddy, sorry you're sad and you have an ouchy on your eyeballs."

I stare back at him in surprise. How can a child of four have such empathy?

When I am sick with nausea like Sam has had, how others feel is the last thing on my mind. I want to be pampered and watch movies. I suck up every drop of sympathy like a sponge. But this child, whose body is wracked with seizures and vomiting, looks in my wet eyes and knows.

The next morning, I come upon Lori, up before all of us, her heart-shaped face fixed in concentration.

She pares delicate slices of apple, staring at her scale. They're a half gram too heavy. She takes a tiny bite from one to bring it in line.

She weighs a square of turkey breast the size of a postage stamp, slices a sliver away, and the scale's immovable justice is satisfied.

Then she places a small glass cup on the scale, gently dips her wrist, and a dollop of oil hits the mark. One more of Sam's meals is born.

I'm just a clown with a mop. But my wife is a priest at a sacrament. Six times a day she takes the concrete and common, and molds and measures and makes the cure. Back aching, she breaks the bread and pours the wine and prays that this mystery would finally be brought down to earth.

What wouldn't you give to heal your child? This cure takes everything in its brutal exchange. To reverse the horror will exact a cost. Hours of measuring. Days of batch cooking and freezing. The glacial pace of Sam's eating. All of it is a robbery of time. But this is the last chance he has.

To bring life to my son, she will put to death countless things. The exquisite jewelry that she makes by hand, books she loves, her beloved solitude — nearly everything she enjoys is abandoned in the balance.

She herself is still recovering from childbirth, yet she pours oil into these wounds. And even as these greasy creations get on Sam's shirt, they are leaving a mark in unseen places.

"This diet has stained my soul," she says one day, her eyes welling up.

I try to make one of the recipes but Lori says that she wants to take the lead on it. Besides, I've got to get back to work. The long hospital visit, new kinds of food, frequent blood labs — all of it has climbed into tens of thousands of dollars. So I shamble off to my office, shot and on autopilot. Blink through emails, try to win new clients, and survive the body blows to my checkbook.

Wondering where we are going to live, Sam's chronic vomiting, grieving Jack — I can't shovel fast enough. Something is filling up inside of me.

One day I'm at work and I suddenly double over like the wind has been knocked out of me. I'm not sick. I have no other symptoms. But it keeps happening. Every week, some kind of emotional dry heave washes over me without warning. I steal away to the office balcony, curses and prayers choking out of me, "Do you hate us? Why don't you do something?"

And then, amid the crash of seizures, nausea, and loss, came an antidote unlooked for.

FOUR
SHELTER

Cooper. We both just like the sound of our new baby's name. And somehow his laughter is making all the badness run backwards.

I call him our "joybird." Through all the running for bowls and holding Sam through another episode, this child of peace just smiles. And I love the meaning of his name: "maker of barrels." We've been poured out and this little boy is pouring himself in, and giggling like he himself has been at the whiskey and the rye.

Nine months before, Lori had left a positive pregnancy test for me to find on the bathroom counter and had written on the mirror, "God is faithful."

And while I hadn't had a spare brain cell to look up the meaning of his middle name, *Lee*, it comes to embody another blessing. Lee was Dad's father who I had never known, and who had helped build our family's first house. And a week after Cooper Lee arrived through a vale of tears, we got the news: our old Spanish home with the crumbling stucco could be ours. Our landlord had decided to sell.

And one meaning of the name *Lee*? "Shelter."

Both my sisters fly in from Chicago to hold Cooper and make meals. Do smelly laundry and change three boys' diapers. And soften the emergencies; Sam seizes one day and hits his head on the corner of a kitchen cabinet. My sister, Sarah, tranquil as ever, looks at his forehead and says matter of factly, "That will be stitches." But now there is someone else to drive to the ER. Life isn't going sideways like a sputtering plane.

And slowly, a more substantial peace is starting to take hold, one that we haven't known since Sam was nine months old.

Recipes like raw coconut oil mixed with peanut butter are doing what five pharmaceuticals in over three years hadn't been able to: bring calm to the high voltage inside Sam.

Three months into the ketogenic diet, the amount of daily seizures were down by two-thirds — thirty a day had dropped to ten. And now, eight months into the diet, we've had six straight days with no seizures. That's never happened.

Maybe my broken prayers are finally being answered. Sam thought so.

"Mom said God help Sam's seizures," he says to me one day.

The brush fires still flare up, but the wildfire is getting contained. Lori's tireless measuring is having an effect — and an effect on her. Nursing Cooper is a dim, inadequate metaphor: all mothers pour themselves into their children. But if Sam's seizures continue to abate, there will be no weaning him from this hellish, heaven-sent diet.

As long as it worked, Lori marked the days by the tenth of a gram.

But I measured mine in jumbo boxes of diapers. None of the three boys were potty trained.

FIVE

BRICKS OF COCAINE AND A
MING VASE

In the predawn light, one-year-old Cooper sings some baby talk to himself. I walk stiffly toward the soft orange glow of the wet-wipe warmer. It's empty.

I find the wipes in the closet, white, sealed, and stacked neatly, like bricks of cocaine. They may as well be blow for how many we're burning through.

I pick up Cooper. He nestles his head onto my shoulder and I whisper-sing a little lullaby. His nose fits in the curve of my clavicle like a key in a lock. Best feeling in the world.

I lay him down on the changing table, take a cold wet wipe from the new pack, apply it to his backside, and — just how loud is a baby's scream? According to our government, my child's cries should be prohibited by law.

The US Department of Labor has determined that 90 decibels (dB), what you hear standing next to a Harley Davidson, is the most a worker should be exposed to for a full eight hours. Now, every five decibels doubles the regulation; exposure to 95 dB (a lawnmower) is allowed for four hours; 100 dB (a power drill) just two hours. And a screaming baby? By one study, he belts out 117 dB (an ambulance siren), which explains my boys' delight at fire trucks: they speak their native tongue.

In fact, the chemistry department at one university reported that 110 dB is "average human pain threshold."

Back to the soft light of the baby room: the pain threshold has arrived. Cooper lets me know, with glass-shattering volume, that wipes should be warmed in the electric warmer, which my mother would conclude is the end of civilization.

And she'd be right. Because if the coddling starts this early, if we as parents admit, in baby talk, that a fresh wipe is "oh-so coldy-cold," then what will our children conclude? What's their takeaway when, from their youngest age, we've not only wiped their butt, but done it with a moist, warm caress?

I'll tell you. Some of these children now populate college campuses looking for a warm feeling called a "safe space." And when they cannot endure a dissenting argument and spew their opinions with all the thought of a bowel movement, then matters have come full circle, if you will.

Our forebears, the hardy pioneers traversing our continent, did not have wet wipes. They had rashes. Especially the parents.

Two hundred years later, I head out the door with all three boys to give Lori a break. I look in the diaper bag to check my wet wipe stash. I weigh one brick in my hand. How many are really in there? Two lousy sheets?

So I head to Costco. On a Saturday. Because a lack of sleep causes all manner of poor decision making. And because nothing absolves parenting desperation like buying in bulk.

While there, yet another stranger strikes up a conversation.

"Oh, I remember when mine were that small!" The kindly woman in her sixties tilts her head, gazing. "It goes by fast."

Finley hits baby Cooper with a brick of cocaine.

"Not fast enough," I mutter in reply.

And what slows time to a crawl? PBS television. Hell is a place where the same episode of *Thomas & Friends* plays on repeat because my three-year-old, Finley, will only sit on the practice potty if he can watch said show.

We're back home now and I'm staring catatonic at a little wooden man on TV. He wears spats and a cravat. He speaks, but his mouth does not move. He exhorts the engines to be "useful." You know what would be "useful," PBS? If the trains went pee-pee.

Both Finley and Sammy sit on their potties watching. I ask them to pray about going pee-pee in the potty. Yes, God has other things to deal with — ISIS, famine, PBS programming — that easily rival the pathological lying I've descended into as I do a fake happy dance over the day's output from Sam: a teaspoon of urine in the bottom of the practice potty.

But Finley's bladder has the capacity of a Ming vase. Later that night, Finley "gets the feeling" and pees in the bathtub.

According to our pediatrician, boys "just learn later," and I had three boys, which translates into fifteen diaper years, or about $20,000 in nappies and wipes. Say it with me: *holy shit.*

I should've listened to Lori.

ONE DAY when she was pregnant with Sam, Lori came home with a sample of Fuzzibunz. Fuzzibunz look like Superman briefs with little snaps. Inside, they employ a machine-washable cloth liner.

Lori plopped down next to me on the couch, rubbed the Superman brief up against her cheek, and made sounds like she was in a softener commercial.

"Honey, they'll be so soft on his skin," she implored.

"Babe," I said, "right now, he is swimming in amniotic fluid. When he gets out here, anything short of a warm bath is going to feel like sandpaper."

"But look how cute they are!"

"How much?" I asked.

"They're about $1,500 for the set."

Lori made the argument that we'd start to save money by the second kid; since we'd reuse the Superman brief and the liners, we wouldn't have to buy more Pampers.

But, raised by children of the Great Depression as I was, I have some fixed financial categories. I don't buy new cars. Almost any kind of debt is bad. And, by all that's holy, I don't shell out fifteen Benjamins for a superhero outfit for my little man to crap in.

So I took a pass on the Fuzzibunz. But that's not where it ended. One night we were invited to listen to the pitch of yet another vendor of guilt-free nappies.

It was a hipster mom and her husband — sorry, *partner*. Their little number was somewhat like Fuzzibunz, but you could flush the liner down the toilet.

But before you do, she explained, one must tear up the dirty liner. With your hands.

So I raised my hand, as anyone would when they've been asked to take excrement-soaked material and tear it in strips.

She responded blithely, "You just tear them up before flushing."

"But," I stammered, "they're filled with poop."

"It's really not a problem," she replied dismissively. You could smell her superiority. Her glare said it all: I didn't care about landfills.

No, I cared about my kid.

I get it: we don't want our landfills to seep into underground aquifers and that toxic water getting to our children.

But toxins are exactly what I'm going to get all over my child as I tear up a liner and then pick him up.

No? I can just leave the child on the changing table as I stroll to the bathroom? The baby will just stay where I left him as I wash my hands?

Oh, these Pharisees had their morality, but I'm relatively sure they never had babies.

So we bought biodegradable diapers. And let me tell you, they have a fascinating feature that absolutely guarantees less fecal matter from ever reaching a landfill: they leak. They biodegraded as soon as they touched my son's skin. So we bought the generics from Target.

So, go ahead, Earth Liberation Front, firebomb my house with alcohol-soaked copies of this book. When I bought my last hundred bricks of wet wipes, I didn't apply the proper emollient of conscience. I was complicit in whatever was coming off the backside of that container ship as it brought those million Costco pallets to our grateful shores.

Sorry, I've got bigger boats to float. I gotta keep a weary wife

143

stocked in red wine and flowers and, no, I don't know if either one is "fair trade."

I'm sorry that my family has contributed our one-millionth portion to some big hole in the ground. Sorry for using anything that can't be composted. Because I just don't have room for your guilt in my garbage truck of care.

My existential reality is a bit bigger than your landfill. The whole wide world my children now inhabit is this quarter acre of dirt under a sunflower sky as Lori's garden grows overhead. And I sherpa its mortgage around every damn day.

Go ahead, drop a dime on me. Because Finley just dropped a penny into Cooper's mouth. The pediatrician says he'll pass it by sometime tomorrow.

So I'm plugging in the wet wipe warmer, stuffing it with a fresh brick, and heading to bed. Because these days, I'm paying through the nose.

SIX
STICKS AND STONES

I start to find them everywhere.

Some are just pebbles and some are stones the size of his fist. They line our window sills. Peer over the edge of the bookshelf. And pile up by our front door like shoes outside a Chinese family reunion.

Rocks.

One night before bath time, Sam digs in his shirt pocket, certain as a saint that there is something down there. He draws out a shred of stone no bigger than a fingernail and carefully puts it to one side.

Rocks are brought to preschool, the kitchen table, and bed. In the morning, I find Sam presiding over a low table in the backyard. He's set dozens of rocks in lines, facing him.

"You okay, rocks?" he asks. "You okay."

He walks away from the table through the ground cover, down a path that Lori has bounded by smooth, softball-size rocks half-buried in mulch. Sam crouches down, moves his fingers beneath one of these baby boulders, heaves it up, and waddles to the low table.

His little stones are now dwarfed by this newcomer. He looks down on them like Caesar presiding over the Senate. I want to imagine that he's welcoming this member into the clan. That his imagination is like any kid's.

But no. That make-believe is all my own; as he addresses the assembly, I can tell something is off with my five-year-old.

A jumble of words comes out of him, but no real sentences. His words aren't just mixed up. It's not just that the phrasing is simplistic. It's not even toddler talk. It's completely opaque.

For over four years, all our energy has been spent trying to contain the epilepsy. The long-sought sanity has finally arrived. And now, as entire days are finally strung together without a seizure slicing them in two, I've begun to pay attention.

The keto diet has brought Sam into a safe harbor, but his mental state has cast off for the deep. My mind drifts to the scenes I've seen.

The neighbor kids try to play with Sam but soon give up when they realize that he can't understand basic games like tag.

At random moments Sam squawks, over and over.

And asking him a question gets me a blank look. And if he answers at all, his words don't resemble the question.

But what he says to his rocks is a hint: "You okay? You okay."

It's the words we've said a thousand times, caressing his face as he would come out of seizure: "You're okay, Sammy, you're okay." But the rest of Sam's speech — if you can call it that — doesn't have that touching antecedent.

As his nonsense phrasing piles up like the rocks in every corner of our home, it's inescapable. Sam is not okay.

———

WE'RE over a year into the keto diet. A few months into the relative quiet of a seizure only occurring several times a week.

But every day, rocks infuse Sam's speech. Ask him almost any question, and "rock" is used as a subject, object, or both. I try to break the code. He's not using the rocks for make-believe. They are not pets, don't have names. Sam doesn't play house with them. But they're something to Sam — what is it?

Sam's otherworldly ways don't stop there. For example, he cannot simply get into the car. When he does finally make it out of the house, Sam plants himself in the front yard, staring down the minivan for ten minutes. No matter how much we implore him with the promise of a favorite destination — his grandpa's house, the local Target — Sam won't move.

Warning him about consequences makes no difference. Picking him up and carrying him to the van results in hysterics. And once we get to where we're going, he won't get out.

Lori takes the kids to a park to meet up with other moms, but Sam won't play on the playground. He insists on sitting on top of her. He grabs her face and twists it towards him. Connection with other moms becomes impossible. The girl is already near empty and he drains the lost drop.

ONE OF MY clients has me up to Santa Cruz for a meeting. Early that morning I get off my plane, grab my rental car, and head towards the coast.

I think about Sam and all that we're going through. My brain feels like a clenched fist. Sure, the seizures are nearly gone, but my son seems to have left the premises with them.

I pull over to drop the top on the rented convertible. Tuck my scarf around my neck and turn the heater on high. Route 17 starts its climb, rising west out of Silicon Valley. The narrow four-lane turns back and forth, uncoiling itself through the hills of cypress. Fingers of fog reach across the road.

It's beautiful, but I can't get my mind off Sam. And once again, I hear that still, small voice:

Leave the ninety-nine, and go look for your lost lamb.

I'd heard that phrase in Sunday School as a little guy. Jesus tells this story about a shepherd. He's got a hundred sheep but one is missing. One of the babies. And though he's got ninety-nine, all the shepherd can think about is that lamb, stumbling in the dark.

On Route 17, the dappled light grew brighter as the sun climbed and burned off the fog.

Go look for your lost lamb.

How, God? Where? He's in some kind of orbit around us, but never touching down. Most of the time, he speaks like no other child I've ever heard. And when he sees me come home, he always runs away.

I want to find him, but I don't know where to look.

That weekend, we check him into Sunday School. I carry him onto our church's playground, reassuring him. He buries his face in my tummy, unable to move. As I chat with two of the volunteers, he steals furtive glances around my body.

"Sam," I suggest, "would you like Kathy and Susan to see your rocks?" He digs one out of his pocket and presents it proudly. The shadow passes from his face, he grins broadly, and I kiss him good-bye. He gives me a thumbs up as I go.

I look back. Kids at the church playground are buzzing about, playing and chasing each other. Sam walks slowly, talking to his rock. Even in a crowd of happy children, Sam is alone.

SUMMER VACATION SEEMED like a good idea at the time.

We arrive in Chicago, but Sam can't depart from his fears. We meet up with a college friend at a mall, and Sam's anxiety spikes and won't come down. We try a playground. Sam won't walk up the sidewalk. There is a reprieve at my older sister's house where we stay for a few days; Sam rambles about Sherry's ten acres, digging for rocks under the ancient oaks. And when we go to leave for Michigan, he loads every single one into our rental car like they're diamond ore.

We pull up to Grand Haven to meet up with my little sister, Sarah, and go with her kids to a fair with bounce houses and a petting zoo. Sam throws himself on the ground and won't move.

We're only five days into our vacation and I'm spent. Inconsolable explosions are robbing time with dear friends. We're finally with cousins that our kids see only rarely, and Sam is like an oil well on fire.

That afternoon, we get back to our rental house near Lake Michigan, and something in me gets a nudge to go after Sam.

"Sam," I ask, "would you like to go to the lake with Daddy for some special time?"

"And I take my rock?" he replies, excited.

At the lake, the overcast sky is a watercolor of pale blue and steely gray. The wind is stiff, frosting the rolling lines of waves.

I roll up our jeans. We sit on a fallen tree trunk near the shore. Sam finds a branch ten feet long and drags it next to him.

We wade. Hop on logs like they were balance beams. The waves chase us. And the branch never leaves Sam's hands.

I think about all that he has faced for the past four years: not just the seizures, but the injuries when he'd fall; the rigor of his diet, which he eats without complaint; and the way he soldiers on, even when he's excluded from other kids' games. Through it all, Sam has smiled when he doesn't have words for it, with no friends to play with except his damned rocks.

I realize he's my hero.

Naturally, Sam wants to take the tree branch home with him and then into our rental house. Sandy and filled with bugs, I draw the line and ask him to keep it in the garage, a request which is not well received by Sam.

But I don't care. For a moment, I had my son back.

A moment that, once we return from vacation, feels like it never happened. The intractable behavior returns. The sudden violence, the running away. I'm out of answers.

So I just admit what isn't working. My expectations of obedience aren't working. Direct commands aren't working.

Am I doing everything wrong? I'd been raised by a father who never took kindly to "back-talk." When I was a kid, any disobedience brought a glare from my father that darkened the sun. Far too often, it was rule by fear. And I'm trying to do the same thing.

I start to wonder what it's like to be a five-year-old boy navigating a spinning earth where everyone moves more surely and speaks more quickly. I had forgotten how big the world can feel when you're little. And I hadn't thought about what it felt like for Sam.

And how do his drugs make him feel? I open the cabinet and pull out one of the anticonvulsants. Sam still needs to take them, even with the diet. I put on my reading glasses; the paragraph is dense. Is he suffering from the side effects? It's hard to know. The FDA requires this long list even if the incidence is rare.

But as I read the list, I feel like a jerk. I hadn't taken them into account. His pediatrician once told me, "They just don't know everything they're doing in a body." He said that, apart from cancer meds, anticonvulsants are some of the most powerful they make.

"Loss of balance and difficulty walking," reads the first side effect. And I feel ashamed of all the times I've hurried Sammy and have asked him to speed up. All the times I've lost my patience.

"Dizziness and drowsiness," reads the next one. Sammy always has a desire to lean heavily against me, sometimes with all his weight. I feel embarrassed as I remember telling him not to hang on me.

"Memory problems," reads the last one. How many times have I asked him not to say the same thing over and over, not to nag?

Were the meds causing Sam's enigmatic language, his dark obstinance — and everything else, too? I can't know with certainty about the presence of the side effects. But the absence of my empathy is clear.

I had hoped, with the seizures largely gone, that all would be

151

well. But I am not well. I've been harsh. My tone has been filled with displeasure.

Convicted, I wonder how it feels to tramp around inside his body, being directed by his broken little brain.

And one day as Sam begins one more impossible morning; stands talking to his favorite tree, refusing to get into my car; as every way I'd ever fathered is exposed; I give up. Something in me breaks.

"Oh, God, change me, forgive me," I pray. "Bring my boy back to us, yes. But moreover, bring me back to my boy."

As usual, I had missed what God was trying to say on that cold morning on Route 17: Sam wasn't the only lamb who was lost. I was, too. And I didn't know what to do.

YEARS BEFORE WE MET, Lori had attended Fuller Seminary to get her master's degree. I remember that they also have a counseling program. I call them and ask if they know anyone who can help us understand our little boy.

They think they might. One of their graduates had begun a psychology practice treating kids with autism and their families called Real Connections. Was Sam autistic? I hadn't thought about it.

They come out to see Sam. Their manner is gentle. Understanding. They seem genuinely interested not so much in a diagnosis, but in Sam himself. And as their sessions unfold in our home I begin to pick up on their ways.

When Sam is rude or abrupt, they don't respond in kind. Instead, they reflect back to him how it feels. They appeal to his empathy by expressing with a dramatic voice how what he'd said had hurt. Or they'll use big gestures to express disappointment.

They teach him about others' feelings, but nothing is ever formal. They do it as they play with him and his Thomas trains. They follow him as he interacts with the neighbor kids and coach him conversationally. But they often don't step in. They just get into his groove and speak in a way that he understands. They literally keep everything on his level — hence the name of their therapy, "Floortime."

They're picking up where the rocks left off. And as I observe Sammy, a theory starts to emerge.

Life comes at Sam pretty fast. But his rocks do not jump out of place. They don't dart around like kids on a playground. They don't talk fast and expect him to answer. No, rocks just are. They are comfortable simply being.

They are empty vessels with which he can symbolize his life. I begin to hear, in the fragments of his sentences, that he is trying to structure his world. I hear, buried in the soil of his syntax, about Knott's Berry Farm, where he goes with his grandparents. I hear him mention his "special diet" to his rocks.

Like me, he's trying to narrate in a fog. His rocks are good listeners and I haven't been. I haven't been walking to the rhythms of his life. I've been insisting he walk in mine.

Winning his obedience had become everything to me. And when Sam would not bend his will, I had immediately assumed it was defiance. But what if it wasn't? What if Sam's discussions with his rocks were pointing to something else?

Sam had been diagnosed with epilepsy when he was ten months old. What if, from his earliest memories, Sam had learned that any moment could bring a loss of control? What if, before he had any words for it, he knew that sovereignty over his own body could be ripped from him in an instant? Hell, one of the first words we taught him was "seizure."

Sam knew, above all else, that the next minute could not be trusted. Most of Sam's five years had been punctuated, up to thirty times a day, by a bizarre invisible force that would throw his body to the ground. Up until this year, Sam's seizures had come so frequently that he might associate anything with their awful power. No wonder transitions to anywhere, to anything, were hard. Transitions meant something new, and new things, or at least sudden things, almost always meant something bad.

But his rocks — they are serene. They do not make quick movements. They can be counted on.

So like them, I start to move slower. Rather than make demands of Sam, I start to make requests. I give him more choice when I ask him to do something.

And, taking a page from the Floortime folks, I begin to acknowledge his rocks the way Sam does. I learn not to command Sam, but to wrap my request in something valuable to him.

When we need to start dinner and Sam won't come inside, I ask: "Would your rocks like to watch us eat dinner?" Or later that night: "Would your rocks like to hear a story?" And, importantly: "Sam, would you like to show your rock how you go potty?"

A change begins. Something in him gets less stiff. Whereas before he had almost always resisted, he now begins to pause and consider his choices. Slowly, he starts to move a bit more willingly from the minivan to the store and back. It's far from perfect. He still has days where he's immoveable. We still need almost an hour of margin time for any excursion. But something is working.

IT IS FALL NOW. The leaves never change around here like they do back in Chicago. But piled up outside our front door, rocks of many colors make up for the apathy of our trees. Sam has painted many of them in bright hues — greens, reds, blues. He's adorned them with stickers. His collection runs into the hundreds.

Silent and simple, they've listened well. Made Sammy's fingers stronger in his constant clutching. Been persevering companions. Far more than me, in the vagaries of my sorrow and confusion, they have been his constant.

In one of his first recorded utterances in Genesis, God speaks matter into being from nothing:

> *"Let the waters under the heaven be gathered together*
> *unto one place, and let the dry land appear"; and it*
> *was so.*[5]

Creation at its most elemental — earth, magma, rocks. I hear the cliffs part the wind and call forth a howl when we climb Mt. Waterman nearby. On the seashore of El Matador up the coast, I hear their orchestral collision with the waves.

And here, on our quarter acre of dirt where the grass grows sparingly, my son has dug up companions older than time, silent witnesses to those first moments where God called the whole earth into being. It's like they were hidden here, waiting for Sam to find them. As if some glacier, after scraping the nearby mountains into shape, had a special delivery for a little boy who would show up many millennia later.

What did Jesus say once? That if praising voices were silenced, "the stones will cry out"? Indeed, they have.

But what if Sam can't? Will he be mute just like them? And what if all these crazy behaviors aren't crazy at all, but just a little boy upset with the fact that his thoughts are foggy? What if the same meds that are holding the seizures at bay are holding back Sam?

No one can tell us if the damage is done, or can be undone. Is his mental condition due to three years of seizures? Would he have been this way had the epilepsy never come? That Sam is behind his peers is a fact today, but what about tomorrow?

Is there a pathway out of this canyon? Can he catch up? Or is he destined to be on the backside of every developmental curve and spend his life looking up an unscalable slope?

SEVEN
MOONLIGHT AND SHADOW

I believe that suffering will be healed and made up for.
That in the world's finale at the moment of eternal
harmony, things so precious will come to pass that it will
suffice for all hearts, for the comforting of all resent-
ments, for the atonement of all the crimes of humanity, of
all the blood that they've shed; that it will make it
possible not just to forgive but to justify all that has
happened.

FYODOR DOSTOYEVSKY

I'm putting the two older boys down. It's our typical night, looking at my father's old aviation books and learning the names of airplanes. Finley falls asleep. But Sam, nestled at my side, is still awake.

I can see a glow through the curtains. I ask Sam if he'd like to see the moon. And he replies in his simple, deliberate way, "I would."

I walk to the window and pull back the curtain. Moonlight saturates the yard next door in a metallic sheen, as if Bogart and Bergman are about to step into the scene. Sam comes and stands next to me on the bed, leaning heavily on my shoulder. High above, the moon creeps westward, mother-of-pearl in a perfect circle.

Sam peers up and the silver light catches his face. Then he puts a question to God, the same question he'd asked his rocks.

Sam waves toward the sky and says, "You okay, God?" And then, satisfied that God is, he concludes, "You okay," gets under the covers, and falls asleep.

But I am not okay.

I head outside and walk through our backyard. The soft gray light steals between the branches of the cedar, but my thoughts are in shadow.

I want to know why all this is happening to Sam. I still hate the platitude of "everything happens for a reason" but my thoughts go there anyway.

In my mind, I hold up an old-fashioned scale, the kind with two platters held by chains. On one side, I place Sam and his disability and all his confusion. But what could possibly justify that weight? What can I place on the other side to correct the balance?

I can't let go of my belief in a just God. To let that go invites far larger problems. It takes the axis from the center of the moral universe. Without a just God, my notion of justice is merely human, the collective wisdom of flawed beings. Or worse, just personal and subjective to me.

No, that I even have an issue implies an ultimate, actual justice. But the issue remains. Sam is an embodiment of undeserved suffering. And this cognitive dissonance has been scratching at the back of my mind for most of Sam's life.

I want my beliefs to align. And if I can't do that, I'd like to put everything in a box: construct sturdy theological carpentry, walk inside, shut the door, and lock myself in. But I can't come up with anything that makes sense.

I wonder aloud if the world is just billions of gears turning, and every tragic and horrific event becomes a means by which God draws people to himself. Each event, just a cog in a cosmic wheel so that other wheels turn in kind. In my mind's eye, I lay out the redemption of the world as a giant machine — with my own son crushed between the gears like a mouse trapped in a clock.

Thinking aloud in the dark, I propose that to God.

"God," I say, "if You would put it to me that way, if You would say, 'If Sam suffers, someone else hearing his story will turn to Me.'

"If that was Your proposition, God," I continue, "that it takes Sam and all he is going through to make the world right or make some lost soul come back home ... then I would say to You, 'Okay, but what else do You got? Is that the best You can do?'"

No, even when I can cling to some higher purpose for everything we're going through, even if I believe the world will eventually be set right, roaring through my mind is an invective: *Really? You needed Sam? You couldn't have done it some other way?*

So yeah, I can posit God's own butterfly effect. I can believe that God has everything so precisely connected that everything hinges on everything else. That what Sam endures is fundamentally necessary to a master plan.

And yes, I can imagine some lost person and whatever it is they need to learn from Sam. I can set them up on one side and set Sam on the other. But the platters tip. The scale is broken. All the turning gears grind and then freeze in place. Because he's still my son.

And yes, Dostoyevsky himself had epilepsy. Good for him. I still don't get it.

I go back inside and finish up the dishes. I take a look at the clock. It's midnight, time for Sam's final keto treatment of the day. In hopes of stilling the one or two seizures which still flare up before dawn, the doctors have prescribed a "midnight snack."

I pick up the condiment-sized plastic container from the counter where it's been thawing and walk into Sam's bedroom. I heave him into my lap and grab his little spoon. He sits on my knees and stirs, but doesn't wake, chewing the oily peanut butter mix.

I put my arms around my beloved son, in whom I am well confused.

SAM'S first day of kindergarten comes. We help him get on his backpack and he poses for pictures in our courtyard. He stretches out his arms like an airplane and grins broadly. Actually gets into my car without a lot of fuss. And then I walk him to the wrong door at his school.

The special needs teacher finds us. I give Sam a tight hug and say those words one more time:

"Remember, as you go through life, you're the greatest." He gives me a thumbs up and goes inside with his teacher.

I stumble to the car, hopes and doubts tearing me in two.

I look at the other kids walking with their parents in bright back-to-school colors and new lunchboxes. Sam has a blocky insulated bag filled with the strongest meds this side of chemo.

Most kids have new notebooks. But to Sam, words and numbers are just lines and circles. And stuffed into his backpack are diapers and wipes for the teacher's aide. He's almost six years old yet his own bodily functions are still confusing to him.

"Remember," I whisper, my voice trailing off. The paradox of my father's benediction cuts into me once again.

Remember, as you go through life, you're the greatest.

How did my father even come up with those words? What would make him coin such an extravagant statement, a blessing so unattached from achievement?

Maybe it was in seeing his older brother return from World War II a broken man.

Uncle Lee loomed large in my childhood, but only in the background. I always thought he looked like John Wayne. But just as The Duke faded from the silver screen, Uncle Lee stopped coming around after we moved to the 'burbs.

The year I graduated from college, I went with Dad to visit Uncle Lee in a nursing home. I was well into my study of World War II aviators by then, but I knew little about combat riflemen like Uncle Lee. I'd heard something from Dad about that miserable campaign in the late winter of 1945, marching east through the snow after the Battle of the Bulge. Lee's boots had soaked through. He'd strip off his socks, shove them under his armpits to warm them, pull his boots back on over bare feet, and go right on marching.

On that day in the nursing home, Uncle Lee sat in bed, propped up with pillows. He was just sixty-four, but looked much older, eyes glassy and skin blotchy. I asked him for a story from the war and he didn't look at me. His gaze was fixed as if staring helplessly into a scene he was powerless to change.

"No, Johnny, I can't talk about that," was all he said.

We said our goodbyes and on the drive back home, Dad told me about his brother, the soldier. That in the year when the war finally ceased, his brother could find no peace.

"He came home from Europe," Dad shared, "walked up the steps of our home, and wouldn't say a word. Went right upstairs. He'd only talk to Pa."

Much later, Pa, Dad's father, told him what Lee had confessed. What had happened on that moonlit night on the Belgian frontier.

On patrol, Lee got separated from his unit near the retreating Nazis — or was he already behind those fluid enemy lines? He took cover in an apple orchard and tried to get his bearings. Nearby, he heard movement and saw a small squad of soldiers approaching, but couldn't tell if they were friendlies. He crouched down and squinted through the grayscale landscape. They were now just fifty feet away, but hadn't seen him. His mind raced. Just two generations before, our family had come from Germany; Lee hit on a common name. Aiming his M1 rifle, he called out in his best German accent: "Heinz?" An unmistakably German voice called back, "Yah?" And Uncle Lee fired and kept firing until the voices fell silent. Voices that followed him all the way back home.

That day when he walked up the steps of his boyhood home on Kilbourn Avenue, he had two Bronze Stars affixed to his uniform, recognition for heroism in battle. America had saved the whole world. If anything, greatness was his to claim.

But what nineteen-year-old is prepared to send a few boys like him into eternity? To see their shocked faces in his muzzle flash?

Lee returned not in triumph but in an overwhelming sense of guilt. Consumed with shame, the conquering hero was conquered by alcohol, trying to staunch the cries of dying soldiers echoing through the moonlight.

As his older brother began a descent into addiction, my father watched, helpless.

And maybe, seeing all that, he determined that his own sons and daughters would never measure themselves by fleeting accolades. Maybe the pain that Lee carried drove Dad to tell us that greatness can't be measured in the evidence, but in something that no one can ever take away.

So Dad spoke, over and over, not a recitation of achievement, but a blessing of unwavering belief:

Remember, as you go through life, you're the greatest.

That was why I never heard it after I received some trophy. There were very few of those. He never said it looking at a report card; I wasn't *summa cum* anything.

My father, wisest of sages in a clip-on tie, had set down a marker to follow. And as Sam's years unfolded in a mystery that had no answers, the purity of what Dad had said cast itself like a lifering through the dark.

EIGHT
BEDRAGGLED HOPE

They who dive in the sea of affliction bring up rare pearls.

CHARLES SPURGEON

It's Tuesday night and Sam is carrying around a beat up Richard Scarry picture book. It's been overloved. Loose pages peek from behind the nubbed edges of the cover. And it's about to get another workout. When the boys and I roll the garbage cans out to the curb, Sam carries the book along. When we go out to the backyard and sit down to enjoy the day's last reflected rays, it's still in Sam's arms. Sam used to carry a rock. Some days it's been a stick. Today, it's a book. But he can't read it.

We listen to the crickets and talk about how they rub their legs together. We hear what sounds like a possum rustling in the tangerine tree above us. But Sam seems to miss all of it. He rambles on in his discursive way about the book. The book comes inside when we brush our teeth and is right alongside

Sam during his nightly regimen of swallowing anticonvulsants with a cocktail of omega oil, baking soda, and calcium powder.

Sam lies down in bed, hugging his book. I read the boys a story and then nod off. I come to with Finley and Cooper asleep but Sam still awake, still clutching the book.

I think of how, despite some progress, Sam still clings to compulsions, still needs a crutch of an object to get through a day. Life revolves around Sam but never seems to adhere. His narratives still reside in a small solar system of their own, crowding out what's going on around him. When I speak with other seven-year-olds, I'm struck by how advanced their language and interpersonal skills are. Of course, they aren't advanced. They're just normal.

Feelings flood through me. My memory runs through a thousand days, the years of almost daily seizures before we had it under control. I think of the damage. Of the UCLA brain surgeon who had told us when Sam was a toddler that if the seizures didn't stop he would never catch up.

I am pummeled by what-ifs. What if we wouldn't have walked out of UCLA that first day we were spooked by brain surgery? Maybe we would've found the keto program a year earlier.

For too long, I had accepted what we'd been told. I had bought the numbers. Seventy percent seemed like good odds. I thought Sam would grow out of it.

I chase the memories around in my head. I was passive. I could have done something sooner. I might have saved my son the damage. He might have been normal.

My wife, my friends — everyone has told me that we did our best. But what might have been haunts me, day after day. And no one can grant me absolution.

My rumination ends with despair. This will be our reality. Sam is broken. He'll be permanently behind. And it's my fault.

Sam tosses and turns next to me. After a half hour of that, I give up. I go out to the living room, get out my Macbook, and ask him to lie down next to me on the couch. I've brought a bunch of work home with me.

He asks if I can turn off the light and I say that I need to keep it on so I can work.

Sam says, "You work hard, thank you for that."

"What did you say?" I ask, startled.

"You work hard, Dad, thank you for that."

I bow my head. Sam has surprised me again. His awareness, his gratitude — it's uncanny. With one phrase he has said exactly what I needed to hear.

Maybe his heart — his good, simple, insightful heart — will defy gravity and drag everything else heavenward.

PART FOUR

THE PRIESTESS AND THE CAVEMEN

In order to arrive at what you are not
You must go through the way in which you
   are not.

T.S. ELIOT

ONE

THE REASON FOR EVERYTHING

No children have special needs quite like the siblings of the special needs.

Siblings go undiagnosed. They don't need pills, but they patiently stand there while the pharmacy has you on hold. They don't need diet therapy, but there's no room for them in the kitchen when Mom needs painstaking focus to measure the next keto ingredient. And they always clean up more toys because Sam moves at the speed of molasses.

They don't get the tutors or mountains of patience. They make do around the periphery. They wait in the car while Sam is negotiated into his seat. When Lori asks them to find their brother who, once again, has wandered down the block, they jump on their bikes and go.

And this morning, I hear one of them cry.

I've come to distinguish my boys' cries like an ornithologist in an aviary. This is not a whine, or a war cry. It's not a bloody knee.

Today's cry is spent and annoyed. A cry to the universe of

"Why?" It's from a boy who could deck Sam in an instant, but has decided to hold back.

And the moment I hear it, I know Sam has done his damage and left the scene.

I come into their bedroom to find Finley, six years old, still in his pajamas, his big Lego star cruiser in a dozen pieces all around him. He is crumpled next to the wreckage, crying into the rug.

I pick him up and hold him in my lap. I tell him I'm sorry. I tell him that Sammy was wrong and that it really sucks. And then I pick up one of the wings and say, "What if this piece goes on the back?"

"No, that's NOT how it goes, Dad!" he snaps, still crying.

I keep him in my lap and pick up another section. "Or we could try this piece on the front of the fuselage."

"Well, that *could* go there, but it's better *here*," he retorts, recovering his mojo.

I offer a few more aerodynamic suggestions and Finley gives my ideas a hearty critique as he reassembles it.

Sam, eight years old, sticks his head in the room and says: "You happy," his go-to when it's abundantly clear that no one is happy.

"No, I'm not happy, Sam."

"You are," he insists.

"What should you say to Finley?" I ask.

"Finley, I forgive you!"

And so the cycle goes: The crime. The half-contrition. The consequence, if I have the energy for it. Then everyone settles back into an uneasy normalcy, waiting for the next go-round.

Daily, Lori tries to read aloud to the boys. Sam pulls on her neck. She asks him to stop and he only digs in further, placing a different book on top of the one that's being read.

Every so often, there are flashes of brilliance, sure. When he says those spooky-accurate things that happen to be what I need to hear, I am in awe for days.

But then the moment is gone, and Lori, his brothers, and I are back in the mire of his mania as he pushes anyone who brushes up against him. Pinches with a ferocity that leaves bruises. And wears a face so closed that nothing I say will open him up.

After one morning of reading that was largely ruined with his interruptions, Lori got a reprieve when Laura, one of Sammy's play therapists, showed up for some Floortime.

Sitting back down in the living room, Lori empathized with Cooper and Finley.

"I'm sorry that it's hard, guys, but we're in this together. And God has Sammy in this family for a reason."

"What's the reason?" Finley instantly shot back.

Man, did he nail it. Aren't we all saying that, to God or anyone who will listen?

And in the meantime, everyone around Sam is shoved into the tiny world of his insistent, repetitive acts. That's a very small place for his two brothers to live. The cramps set in.

TONIGHT AT DINNER Sam once again picks up the mantle of defiance. I ask him to sit in his chair. He won't. And when he finally gets settled, he pulls one butt cheek off the edge of the

173

chair, and looks at me over his cheekbones. Then he throws his food on the ground, which invites the unique pleasure of pulling out a spatula, scraping up every ounce no matter where it's fallen, and putting it back on his plate.

I carry him to his room for a time-out and then come back into the kitchen to resume eating with the boys. Lori leaves to go walking with a friend.

"You know guys, we're all working on things," I say to the boys. "Sammy is working on obeying Mommy and Daddy."

"And I'm working on not whining," interjects Cooper.

"And I'm working on not potty talking," says Finley, who then adds: "And, Dad, you're working on not yelling."

We all laugh. My two little men have found a beat in this off-rhythm family and given the snare drum a rimshot.

How did they know the right thing to say? It is more than humor. It is a grace that allows them to laugh. It is perfect, except for one thing: Sam can't enjoy the moment with us. He isn't here. Is he ever really here?

Oh, he's there, just outside the kitchen. I can hear him putting a toe outside his time-out, quietly listening from the hallway.

He undoubtedly hears the laughter. But does he know what it means? Because I don't know what anything means to Sammy anymore.

So let me say this: I am special needs.

I don't know how to not react when he goes off without warning.

I don't know how to recover in time and say what I want to say, which is that I delight in him. I delight in his smile and his

174

quirky play where he decapitates his Lego men and stacks the heads like a skinny Nordic totem pole.

I don't know how to reconcile a boy who prays so constantly yet is so hurtful. I don't know how to move towards him when almost every time I come home, he runs and hides.

I don't know what to do with my anger when I snatch him out of a busy street that he's run into and he responds with clawing fingernails that leave bruises.

And, yes, I can gather these two brothers of his, coach their soccer teams, carve out adventures for them, and make sure they get time where they are seen, heard, and know they are loved. I can do all that.

But I don't know how to handle these new seizures that convulse our whole family. While the horrifying actuality of epilepsy is now more rare, Sam's erratic behavior seizes our days.

This boy tears a line through the peaceful firmament of the bluest sky on our best day and leaves us with Finley's unanswerable question, hanging in the air:

"What's the reason?"

TWO
WELCOME TO THE NUDIST COLONY

I come home to the sound of pounding feet. Finley, age six, on a detour from the bathtub and stark naked, rumbles down our long hardwood hallway like a bowling ball. Cooper, age four, also adorned in his birthday suit, follows close behind, a tight grin of baby teeth all grown in. These streaking comets tip me over like a tackling dummy, describing their private parts with the chattering rapidity of courting squirrels.

I pull Finley and Cooper off of me and take a closer look. Magic marker is drawn all over their faces and limbs as if the Cat in the Hat had dropped by and taught them Maori body art.

Sam, age eight, peeks out at the end of the hallway. Actually, one foot peeks out. Then one hand emerges, holding out a stick. Then the other hand points to it. But I still haven't seen his face.

This is his daily, slow reveal when I arrive home. He hides behind his favorite tree in the front yard. Or just turns his back. I try to be cerebral about it. Try to chalk it up to his banged up nervous system assimilating another arrival. But I know I'm just guessing. Still grasping at rationales so I don't take it personally.

Or maybe he's keeping his distance because his brothers are not done with their native greeting. They walk away from each other a few steps as if preparing for a duel. Facing away from each other, they bend over, and with a shout of battle that rivals William Wallace, run backwards at each other, jousting with their bare butt cheeks. As the flab clashes, potty words spew forth like a Roto-Rooter in reverse, each reference to their personal plumbing punctuated by peels of giggling.

"Too loud," Sam says as he comes up to me.

As usual, Sam is right. But how have these creatures learned such behavior? Into the long debate of "nurture versus nature" I lay my ace: My wife and I have never sprinted around the house naked. Not in front of them anyway.

No, bathroom humor is God's fault. When fashioning Adam's large intestine, he knew full well that he was providing the raw material for subsequent millennia of toot jokes, from *The Canterbury Tales* to *Dumb and Dumber*. And behold, it was very good.

"They're running," Sam says matter-of-factly.

Indeed, there they go, heading for the back door, against my pleas to start their bath.

I am a traffic cop to a track team on crack.

Sam raises his index finger to the side of his head, wiggles it, and says, "Loco," the shorthand his grandfather taught him to explain his brothers. I glance back at the nudists.

"Do not bounce the chickens on the trampoline!" I bellow out the backdoor.

Mid-bounce, Finley throws the chicken off. She flaps down and struts away, only too grateful to be freed from the clutches of this Spartan farmer.

"Guys, five more minutes, and then you have to get in the bath."

Have I lost my mind? *Five minutes* is: "That thing Dad says before he really means it."

As his two younger brothers do their best Cirque du Soleil, I look back at Sam. He is quietly collecting twigs throughout our yard.

"Dare's one dare," says Sam, picking up another stick the size of his little finger. ("Th"-words such as "there" come out as "dare," "this" as "dis," and so on.)

Some sticks are several inches long, others no larger than a toothpick. He carefully hunts and bends, clutching the tiny bundle of wood in one hand.

Now one of the exhibitionists is crying. The cage match has someone "pinching my pee-pee, Daddy!" I corral them through the backyard, and Cooper says, "Dad, do you know what a chemical reaction is? Can we have one in our bathtub?"

I turn the water on and go back outside.

"Hey bud, it's time for a bath," I say to Sam.

Sam turns his head away and wags his index finger at me: like the last thousand times, a direct request from me will not be considered.

I forget so quickly. Sam can't move from scene to scene like we do. He'd like nothing to be as sudden as a seizure, thank you.

I pick up one of the sticks lying nearby.

"Sam, would your stick like to watch you take a bath?" I ask, twirling the twig between my thumb and forefinger.

"It would," Sam agrees. But his stick is not the magic wand I'd

179

hoped. It's a tricky business to jump in, mid-song, to the slow dance that is Sam.

He goes on a verbal jag for a few minutes, a description crowded with definite articles like "dat" and "dare," but no real nouns.

Sam finishes and reaches with his hand for mine. I shepherd him to the bath and he puts each stick. On the counter. With the speed. Of. This. Sentence.

Sam gets in and the water crests over the edge. I ask Finley and Cooper to get out but that just incites an argument. So I ask each boy to guess a number between one and ten.

"B!" says Sam.

"Sammy, that's a letter. Let's try guessing the color I have in mind instead."

"S!" Sam says.

Sam's mix up leaves me crestfallen. Recent testing placed him at a "low kindergarten" level, but I know kindergarteners who know their letters and numbers. What's going on? You'll have to ask the team of scientists who are on a first name basis with him.

A speech therapist works with him for two hours every week. Sam is logging a "one-percentile" — he's failed every baseline.

An occupational therapist helps Sammy with his balance and his grip. Buttoning one button on his pajama top might take Sam ten minutes.

There's tutors. Resource teachers. The UCLA team who oversee Sam's diet therapy.

There's an unbelievably patient tae kwon do instructor. Our cheerful, bright babysitter who knows how to mix Sam's medicines. Devoted grandparents who take the kids out every week. And friends who pray us through.

But not one of them can tell us if the next few years will see progress. No one can tell us what will become of Sam.

THREE
THE FATHER, THE SON, AND THE HOLY TOAST

I push their limbs through mismatched PJ's and herd them to the dinner table.

From their earliest memory, children are conditioned to get food when they demand it and that divine right dies slowly.

Lori endured long nights of nursing each boy through their first year. They'd fall off her like drunken seamen rolling down a listing deck — and then spit it back up.

Mother's milk is brilliant, an unreproducible mixture that chemically adjusts to the age of the child. Its antibodies actually change their chemical makeup as the child grows. My children preferred dirt.

So it's not that my two younger children won't eat. Quite to the contrary, they regularly chew on Play-Doh and each other. But anything they liked the day before? Anything they said they'd eat fifteen minutes ago? No way.

Now, I haven't actually said, "Eat your food, children are dying in Calcutta," because my children's knowledge of geography only extends to the Island of Sodor, where Thomas the Train lives.

"Disgusting!" Finley says trenchantly to some delicious, sautéed chicken breast my wife has prepared. I stare at my six-year-old. Where did he learn that word?

And like they've rehearsed it together, Finley and Cooper both purse their lips, put their faces near their plates and then look up, noses crinkled. Sam stares at both of them, contentedly chewing the avocado from his keto menu.

If anything, Sam has a right to complain about the repetitive nature of his diet. But the other two acting like foodies? They both chew on their bedspreads.

ANOTHER DINNER TRADITION I have bungled is the blessing. Lori had a nice idea: with a Sharpie, we write the names of friends, family members, and missionaries on popsicle sticks. The kids choose a stick and that's their prayer for the night. Sweet idea, right?

Except it's a disaster. First, the kids disagree on who gets to pray first. And then the one who doesn't pray first whines through the other's prayers. Because if there's anything you want kids to understand about prayer, it's who *wins*. And then Sam prays and goes on. And on. Praying for Sir Topham Hatt, a fat man in a morning coat and spats who doesn't exist.

But at least their theology is solid. Tonight, Finley wrapped things up with: "In the name of the Father, the Son, and the holy toast."

I glance at the clock. It's just past eight. What Lori needs most is to wake up to a house whose contents don't appear to have been blasted by a cyclone.

But expecting a child to clean up his toys is like asking W.C. Fields to stack cases of brandy. Every toy Cooper picks up holds mystical promise. Time is still a bit elastic in his four-year-old brain. "Dad, a long time ago," he says, referring to last week, "I was playing with this toy, and now I've found it."

And then there is the noise. They cannot simply put toys away. They have to push their buttons. And each toy takes its pound of sanity before being retired to the toy box.

Finley picks up a large school bus, pushes the button, and I hear churlish laughter like a bag of chipmunks being dumped into a pitching machine.

Cooper goes to put away his tugboat and I hear a sing-song medley as if twenty children had all been loaded with maple syrup and then squeezed at the same moment.

They also have vehicles which gain energy from my children shaking them. Some sensor inside these "shake cars" — which could have been used, I don't know, in a life-saving medical device — "knows" when they are being shaken, and when the cars are set down on our floor, away they go.

But they don't go away. The toys talk, loudly. One clownish hot rod is the getaway vehicle of the Joker. I hear a cackle that rivals the Wicked Witch and I'm sure can be heard in Kansas: "YOU'RE DONE FOR NOW, BATMAN!"

Sam looks up at me. "Too loud," he says.

I shut the door to the hallway and guide Sam to the living room, where their wooden blocks need to be returned to a large canvas box. I help Sam sit down nearby and he carefully sets down his sticks. I shove the blocks across the floor so they're within arms' reach.

"Dis one goes dare," Sam begins, and lifts one block into the box. Sam's motor thus started, I turn back to the boys.

The crowded contents of their bedroom are now spilling into the hallway. The chore has gone backwards, shake-cars flying past school buses in a cacophony of Satanic verses.

I walk into the kitchen to mix up Sam's evening meds and then go back to check on his progress.

Softly narrating his movements, Sam methodically picks up each wooden block. I pause to watch him. His persistence is undaunting. The pile of blocks is nearly done.

"Sam, great job, buddy!"

"I did dat, I did dat DARE!" he proudly proclaims.

"Sammy, can I pick you up and carry you to your syringes?"

"You can," Sam replies, slowly accepting the next move of the shifting dance floor.

I carry Sam to the kitchen, sit him on the butcher block, and hand him the 8 mL syringe. He sets his sticks to one side, places the syringe in his mouth, points it toward the sticks, places both hands on either side of the plunger and pulls them together.

Sam swallows and says, "I sick." I flinch, memories of our year of nausea snapping me to attention. How quickly can I get Sam to the toilet?

We've been on the keto diet for a few years now. Sam isn't supposed to throw up anymore.

"Sam, you're okay," I say, not really believing it.

I walk Sam to the bathroom. Tell him to stop leaning so far over the toilet; I don't want the power of suggestion to take over. I keep hoping the digestive drug he's just taken will settle his tummy and allow the anti-seizure medication he just swallowed to get into his system. After a minute he concludes, "I better."

I carry him gingerly from the bathroom, trying not to stir whatever pot is boiling down below. I throw some old beach towels on his bunk and set him down. I ask the boys to pray with me for Sam to feel all better.

We finish praying but I'm still on edge. Sam looks at me and says, "Be brave."

What?

"You be brave, Dad."

THEY DROP off to sleep and I walk down the hall shaking my head. How does this boy know what to say? He doesn't get the difference between a color, a letter, and a number — but gets everything else? I'm not so brave, and he knows it.

"Sammy the Brave." That's what I called him during his earliest visits to the hospital. What I still say when he's poked during his regular blood labs. I know of no one braver.

Yet to say that Sam is a saint with a bad circuit board is to miss the rest of it. He still can be maddeningly obstinate. Seating him for a van ride is still negotiated as if he's holding a hand grenade. Without warning, he hits his brothers with shocking severity. He runs away into crowds almost everywhere we go. He got lost at the dinosaur museum the other day. The one with the tar pits. Lori came home, her nerves rubbed raw.

And I wonder: in ten years, when he's eighteen, will I be talking to syringes as if they're sentient as I cajole my son to take his medicine?

I hear parents say all the time how unique their child is. I just want my kid, for one day, to be like everyone else.

FOUR
A DAY IN THE LIFE OF A SCOLD

It's the wee hours of the morning when it comes clacking down the hallway like a freight train over a crossing. *Click-clack, click-clack.* It's "Luke," his one wonky wheel giving him that old-timey charm on our hardwood floor.

Sam started talking about "Luke" a couple of months ago.

"Where is Luke?" he'd say. When we asked him who "Luke" was, he'd change the subject, or point to the garage. The obtuse charade continued for a few weeks. Then Lori told me, "Luke is my suitcase."

Like everything else, Sam's christening of Lori's old black roller bag had come out of nowhere. Sam doesn't know anyone named Luke. He hadn't watched *Star Wars.*

It's 4:00 a.m. I wake to the sound of Luke and hope I can get to Sam before he wakes Lori.

I intercept him in the hallway. Sam points to the front zipper pockets of the suitcase. These are Luke's "eyes" and "mouth." Much like his beloved rocks of a few years ago, Sam has imbued yet another object with personhood.

I walk Sam to the bathroom and then to my bed, knowing that my sleep for the night is effectively over.

I must have dropped off though, because I hear a four-year-old in full voice, six inches from my ear.

"Dad, are there volcanoes in California?" There's about to be, kid.

In the gray light of dawn, Cooper is standing next to my bed.

"Mmmm, no," I respond, half my face in the pillow. I stumble towards the bathroom and hear a sound coming from somewhere in the house. What is that metallic snap like a cigarette lighter, a "click-click-click" in rapid succession?

I sprint to where Finley is standing at the new stove, turning the knobs.

"What are you doing?" I shout and flip the burner off.

I am more awake now than I have ever been in my life. The parenting advice I've gotten from videos and books is nowhere to be found. For example, that tip that a parent should "Connect before Correct"? No, if I waited to "Correct," the house would burn to the ground.

Instead, I yell. I go on and on, narrating a fireball, the entire house lifting off the ground like a scene in a Michael Bay movie. Finley just stares at me. I'm scared and tired and I'm not a good dad right now. And I hate Michael Bay movies.

That night, I come home from work blasted from stress. Once again, my business is in a downturn. Our little boat is taking on water and I'm bailing all day.

Which is what I find the boys doing in their sandbox. In the idyllic golden light of the early evening sun, sand is being thrown into the air.

And what is that I hear, wafting through my mind? Is it the words of William Blake?

To see a World in a Grain of Sand
And a Heaven in a Wild Flower
Hold Infinity in the palm of your hand
And Eternity in an hour

Nope, sorry. That would be some other father.

Me? I yell across the yard. Because their grandfather, who wheelbarrowed forty bags of sand, has told them not to waste it. And their mother and I have pleaded with them to not spill it over the sides.

"Eternity in an hour"? Yeah, that's how long it'll take to wash the sand out of their hair. And I'm still going to find it in my sheets.

Suck it, Blake. My children don't feel like precious gifts, sent from beyond time and space. I just want them to stop taking up space in my bed.

So I stride over and rant about the sandbox rules. My children look at me blankly. I may as well be explaining the electoral college.

I'm still grumpy when the boys arrive at the dinner table. I don't even give them a chance to complain — or do the right thing.

"Boys, what do we say?" I grouse.

"Thank you, Mommy, for my food," Cooper and Finley reply in unison and fear.

Sam tilts up his head and once again looks over his cheekbones at me. That's his poker tell when he's doing something wrong. He sets a bunch of sticks on the table.

"Sam, we can't have sticks at the table," I say. He looks down his cheekbones again. I ask him to put them on the window sill. More cheekbones.

I glare at Cooper who is sitting with one foot propped near his butt, knee leaning against the table. I tell him to put it down. Then Finley spills his milk.

I wish I could tell you that I paused, mid-reaction, and realized what was happening. Instead, I reenact a scene from my childhood.

My father leaps out of his seat at the kitchen table, and, like the last hundred times, hits his head on the pewter chandelier he'd hung in the wrong place when he'd built the house. His hand shoots up to steady it. Then he sprints to the other side of the kitchen, snatches a dish towel and runs back, angry and upset.

And now I'm the star of the same show. Crying over spilled milk indeed. But I don't hit pause. Don't see where all this has come from and where it's going.

I finish soaking up the milk and seething with annoyance, say, "Do not chew with your mouth open. Hold your mouth over your plate."

I get them into bed, pull *Prince Caspian* from the bookshelf and squeeze between them. Sam turns toward me onto his right side, and loops his left arm tightly into mine. Finley does the same on my right. Cooper crab walks up my body till the back of his head is resting on my chin.

I grumpily inform Cooper that his efforts to see the pictures will make it impossible for me to see the words. I finally start, doing the voice of the good badger, Trufflehunter, in a kind of a high-brow English accent. They interrupt, ask questions; who wouldn't? Narnia is a strange place. But I snipe back at them, telling them to just listen.

Sam drops off, twigs still held tightly in his hand. Cooper leaves his perch at the top of my chest, nestles between my feet and says, "Daddy, tell me when there's a picture." I push through to the end of the chapter and Finley begs me to continue. I remind him that his sleeping brothers will miss it. He tries to wake them. We argue. I turn off the light and he finally drops off to sleep. I get up, gingerly stepping over them.

Lori finds me and gently calls me out. Tells me that dinner has devolved into a recitation of rules. *Put your napkin on your lap, don't belch at the table.* She says she wants their memories of our times around the table to be hearing about each other's day, sharing stories and laughing, not some test of etiquette they always fail.

She's right. I'm a manners cop. I hated it when I was a kid. They hate it now. And it's not just dinner; is there any time left when I am not in some constant stream of corrective? Do I ever break from the dialect of scold?

The whole stupid skit — bath time, dinner time, cleaning up toys — it's a law of diminishing returns. Because one day, they're not going to have me threatening them. If I am teaching them to only act from fear, what happens when I'm no longer there?

I want them to change. I want me to change. But I don't know how to do either one.

Why do they grow up to care about others — or anything at all besides themselves? What changes a heart from wanting its own way?

I have no idea.

But Lori does.

FIVE
I MARRIED AN ARTIST

The fullness of joy is to behold God in everything.

JULIAN OF NORWICH

One day Lori was approached by Finley, then three years old. He took her index finger in his hand, picked his own nose with her finger, handed it back, and walked away.

That is all you need to know about the selfless motherhood of my wife. She is a priestess among cavemen. And one day, she taught them some cave painting.

They took shape slowly. Almost imperceptibly, like so much of my life with her. One day, they just appeared, *ex nihilo*.

It was just butcher paper at first, a long brown cylinder three feet wide. I saw it in the garage and didn't think anything of it.

Then one day when I was at work, she asked each of the boys to cut a sheet six feet long and lay down on it, with their hands raised above their heads. She took out a pencil and helped each of them trace their brother's body. Then she let each of the boys take paint and fill in the outline.

Later that day, I found them taped up our hallway — self-portraits of vivid hue. Each boy had translated himself into an autobiography in tempura.

Sam had painted his right arm and leg in scarlet, the rest of his body in orange, and made the shape of a pale white flame near his belly button. Around his body were streaks of color as if he was on fire.

Cooper's body was flanked with forest green and sprinkled with gold glitter. A volcanic eruption came out of the top of his head like a red rain cloud. And beneath his feet, as if he was going to ride down an erupting mountain on a surfboard, was a dark burgundy wave of flame.

Finley filled the paper, full bleed as we say in my industry. All the way to the edges, a forest of broad brushstrokes was applied in broccoli green, aquamarine, and navy blue. The right side of his body was in red, and the left in a wet pale green, the paint pooling on the paper as it dried.

Would I have done this? Would I have fearlessly put a paintbrush in their paws? No way. But Lori — broad palette, large canvas, freedom to spill. But they didn't spill. Their bodies were clearly visible even though they colored outside the lines.

I got home from work and just stared at them on the wall, amazed. I asked Lori how much she helped.

Pointing to Finley's portrait she said, "I didn't tell them how to do it. It was all them."

The following week, after she explained the circulatory system during homeschool, I came home to find that the three self-portraits had each grown a paper heart: Finley's was painted purple and pink; Sammy, purple and brown; and Cooper chose teal.

I left for work one morning and noticed that they were cutting up one of my old car magazines. And that day, each of them signed their self-portraits in cut-out letters like a ransom note. Perfect.

Then she had them cover their hands in white paint and press them onto squares of brown paper. Those too were cut out and placed on their self-portraits.

I asked her where she had gotten the idea for this evolving, mixed-media wonder — what book or curriculum had she consulted? And she said, "My own head."

And when I look around our home, I realize she graces everything she touches.

She never just hangs something, for instance. She will twist wire into curved fashionings so that adorned atop the most mundane of objects, say, a calendar, is a metallic flourish. I bang a nail and leave a gouge in the plaster; Lori leaves the everyday a bit more beautiful.

From the sandbox she built, to a teepee that grows string beans; from our chicken coop, to the grape arbor, and the wildflowers you'll find growing between them — all of it takes the beauty of the world, shapes it, and brings it into view. Eggs are laid, jasmine softens the air, and the bounty of her vegetable garden fills our table to overflowing.

A FEW YEARS AGO, I noticed that every soup can we owned was being shorn of its label. The empty can with its label of black beans or coconut milk was soaked off, leaving a bare, silver cylinder. They started to stack around the kitchen, but I didn't think much of it.

Then in her office, I found a wood shelf that she had constructed about six feet up. Looking closer, I found writing on it. Lori had glued, in varying angles, pages of a book onto the wood in a pastiche of diagonals and then sealed the pages in lacquer. I looked again and realized it was the first few chapters of the book of Genesis.

And resting atop the words that had made the world were the gleaming bare soup cans, each of them now stuffed with a different tool for my boys. Markers, paint-brushes, colored pencils — every conceivable thing they could grasp for creation was sitting on top of the very story of creation itself.

The symbolism was subtle. At the time, the boys were six, four, and two. They were too short to even see the words, let alone understand the meaning. But Lori is never in a hurry. She knows they'll grow taller. Knows that one day they'll retrieve a paint brush, tilt their head, and read what's been there all along.

How does she do all this? Make things appear, abracadabra? How is it that for ten years I missed it? It's been right under my nose: I married an artist.

ONE DAY, Lori is at a local nursery to replace one of her clay pots when she happens to notice a caterpillar on one of the milkweed plants. Looking at the pudgy creeper in his striped onesie, she gets an idea.

She brings the plant home and relocates the caterpillar to a large mason jar where it soon spins itself a chrysalis. Doing some research, Lori discovers that monarch butterflies feed on, and will only lay their eggs on, milkweed. She plants it outside, and soon, it becomes an airport of orange papery wings as word gets around. Not long after, Lori discovers tiny eggs on one of the delicate branches and gently brings it inside to be the next contestant. Soon, a menagerie of caterpillars begins to set up shop on the kitchen bar.

The first monarch butterfly emerges, its dewy wings still wet from its shorn sleeping bag. Finley and Cooper can't tear their eyes away. Another one breaks through and twirls around, wet wings stuttering. The boys stare in awe.

Almost on a whim, Lori has made space for beauty to occur. She has brought the boys into the orbit of her delight. Anointed a moment. And our boys, these comets with souls, pause and grow quiet, moved by creation in real time.

But not Sam. Nothing registers on his face. It may as well not be happening. Even as we watch the chrysalis pierced by new life, Sam stays in his old one.

The event in front of him has no adhesion. The wonder of the butterflies can't change his daily rut: fifty times a day, like a needle stuck in a battered LP, he repeats a list of objects over and over:

"Surrey bike."

"Bighorn sheep."

"Shuttle bus."

"UPS truck."

… and a dozen more in an endless loop. And no matter what is happening around him, he insists that we print a black-and-white google image of that object and attach it to his clipboard. Then he pulls out his markers and colors over the photo.

I ask him to stop and look. "Sam, the butterfly, he's coming out of his house!" But, like his rocks of a few years ago, nothing else seems to matter.

What is he doing? Like so many steps on my journey with him, it takes me a long time to understand.

These objects he's memorized all have an antecedent; they are all tied to events that happened to him. He knows, for a minute, that things he experienced were real. Papa *did* rent surrey bikes along the boardwalk that day and take Sam for a ride. He *did* travel to Nevada to visit Grampy near Lake Mead, and the bighorn sheep *did* come down the mountain to graze at their local park.

The photo of the object is printed; the travelogue in his head comes to life; reality is confirmed. And for Sam, the precarious world slows and makes sense. He remembers the towering windmills we saw en route to see his great-grandmother. The shuttle buses of film crews who decamp across the street. Or the UPS truck that comes to our house.

And with all the repeated requests, I think he's asking Lori and me: *tell me that what I saw that day was real.* He's laying claim to his memories.

His spinning earth slows for him, but all of us have to revolve around it. He jabs Lori's shoulder. Grabs her phone. Or escapes with her laptop. And Lori finds where Sam is hiding, types "windmills" into the browser and the cycle continues.

And today, when a butterfly had a birthday, I try, like so many times before, to get Sam to realize what he's missing. But no. Even as this nature movie rolls on in full color, Sam insists on a new black and white printout.

As Cooper and Finley stare slack-jawed at the caterpillar's metamorphosis, Sam remains unchanged.

I COME home to find a shallow wooden box resting atop a windowsill in the living room. Inside it are built-in frames, a couple dozen rectangles and squares an inch or two long. It looks like a cross section of a tenement for mice.

In one little square sits a bristling sphere of a seed, a tiny puffer-fish of wood. In the next, there's a winged beetle, its elytra shell an iridescent green. Three tops of three acorns sit nearby, like jaunty little berets.

The boys and Lori had discovered these items on their walks around the block. She wasn't letting them miss a thing. Apprehending beauty requires attention.

Over the next several days and weeks, the cells were filled with new inmates — a feather, some sea shells, a pine cone.

As I pull away one morning, I see them start off on another walk.

Cooper and Finley are as predictable as an electron. They dart about, staring downward. They stalk. Then, quick as a wink, Finley strikes, cupping his hand around a baby lizard. I pause the car and watch Sam. He trails behind, bending and straightening like a sandpiper in slow motion. He picks up a twig, places it in his hand with the care of a jeweler, and moves on.

Maybe the boys see God in all this, or maybe their souls lie fallow. Lori always refuses to delineate their spiritual progress. She knows they are not integers on a number line. She knows the boys only pause for a moment as they skip down the side-walk. A puppy chasing a moth is more reflective.

But Lori is as patient as a season. She lets time do its work. And maybe in some spring of their lives, in the next decade or when we're gone, these memories will come back, sure and true. And the unnecessary, lavish splendor of it all will pose to their minds something they have to answer: why is there beauty at all? Why does the California poppy preserve bloom as if a whole paint factory has exploded? Why do our orange blossoms raise their voices in silent song, scenting our backyard with sweetness every summer?

Like one of her favorite songwriters puts it, Lori has heard "the big music,"[6] the power of God behind everything. And she revels in it. Despite being grounded to the slowness of Sam's diet; despite the mystery of his condition that still has doctors shrugging; despite constantly unpacking the latest wrinkle of crazy that brings many days to a halt; in spite of all that — Lori knows that wonder is a stylus writing an incessant question into the soft clay of their souls.

And under this pressing of beauty, I am slowly changing.

I'm walking around the back of the house when I see Finley, fifty paces off in the farthest reaches of our yard. Framed in the drooping branches of the cedar, he's making a St. Lawrence Seaway in the shallow winding ditch that borders the vegetable garden and the lawn.

The hose near the chicken coop is on full blast as he fills Lake Erie — or maybe he imagines a salmon ladder up the mighty Columbia. He is wholly immersed, hands in the mud. Is there anything like a boy lost in his creation, as if nothing else exists?

I see the gallons gush from the spigot, I think about the water bill, and something correcting almost comes out of my mouth.

Then, thank Jesus, the words stop in my throat, as I think, no, let this sweet movie run in his mind. Wherever he is, crossing the Big Muddy, digging in Panama, let it run, let him be, because these years are rolling away downstream and I can't hold them in my hand.

Nearer the house, seated on the concrete in front of the garage, is Sam.

Something is happening that I haven't seen before. Sam isn't just choosing the right stick, he's setting it down in a pattern.

And not just a pattern but a picture. Longer sticks travel several inches in vertical; thicker pieces frame the outsides; and on the top of these rectangles he's placed two triangles.

I squat down next to him. "Sam, did you make a castle?"

"Bounce house," he replies, a phrase that usually requires a Google image search and a trip to our printer. But not this time. He has gone from obsessing to creating.

He takes another stick and breaks it into smaller bits so he can fill in the details.

I look at his palette in the pile next to him. There's stringy ground cover and black breakage from the pecan tree that leans over the garage.

I pick up one of the sticks with knuckled breaks in the bark, as dead as a bone in Ezekiel's valley.

Son of man, can these bones live?
O Lord God, You know.

SIX
GOD IN PAIN

Now Jesus loved Martha and her sister and Lazarus. So when He heard that he was sick, He then stayed two days longer in the place where He was....

Martha therefore, when she heard that Jesus was coming, went to meet Him, but Mary stayed at the house. Martha then said to Jesus, "Lord, if You had been here, my brother would not have died. Even now I know that whatever You ask of God, God will give You." Jesus said to her, "Your brother will rise again." Martha said to Him, "I know that he will rise again in the resurrection on the last day." Jesus said to her, "I am the resurrection and the life; he who believes in Me will live even if he dies, and everyone who lives and believes in Me will never die. Do you believe this?"

...When Mary came where Jesus was, she saw Him, and fell at His feet, saying to Him, "Lord, if You had been here, my brother would not have died." When Jesus therefore saw her weeping, and the Jews who came with her also weeping, He was deeply moved in spirit and was troubled, and said, "Where have you laid him?" They said to Him, "Lord, come and see." Jesus wept.[8]

THE GOSPEL OF ST. JOHN

Jesus knows that Lazarus is sick, but decides to delay in coming. Well, that's a problem, isn't it?

He lets him die. Both Martha and Mary call Him on it. Because this was not just another sick stranger in some town. No, this was a friend.

When Martha presses Him on His tardy arrival, He tries to bring her back to ultimate reality: "I am the resurrection and the life; he who believes in Me will live even if he dies." But Martha wants to talk about the here and now: "I know that he will rise again in the resurrection on the last day." It's as if Martha is saying, "Yes, that heaven-talk is fine but we hurt today. We are in pain now."

I think that's what I've been saying ever since Sam was diagnosed: what about now? Like Martha, I've said to God: *All right, fine, one day we will shake off this mortal coil and Sam will be perfect in heaven and we'll all be happy. Got it, thanks. Is that it?*

Then the scene shifts.

Mary comes and falls at His feet, weeping the same words: *Lord, if You had been here, my brother would not have died.*

But this time, He does not have the same answer. At first, He doesn't say a thing: "He was deeply moved in spirit and troubled." Then He only says, "Where have you laid him?" And then breaks down Himself.

Why does the almighty one, the one who knows the outcome, cry? He had let it happen. He knows what's coming, knows He's going to raise Lazarus from the dead. And yet He's torn apart. What is going on?

He who could dwell in unassailable solitude, the one who, if He chose, could mute every voice of sorrow and have no cry of torture ever come to His ears — this one, has opened Himself up to feeling pain. In entering into friendship with Lazarus and his two sisters, He has made Himself vulnerable.

On that moonlit night in my backyard a couple years back when I posited to God my machine with a million gears, the suffering was all on our side. It was Sam and those who loved him who were in pain. I wanted a justification for what we were going through.

But what if my ledger is one sided? Jesus breaks down and falls apart in Mary's arms. He chose to experience pain. Chose to know the depths of grief. What if the same is true of Sam? What if God could lessen His own pain by taking away Sam's condition, but is instead at the bedside of my little boy, weeping? Not impotent, but convulsed with sorrow.

If God is here, if God is present and knows the pain of Sam — every bruise and cut when he collapses, every befuddled look when he doesn't understand playground games, my every stab of dread about his future — if He feels it all and yet still decides to allow it to happen, that changes everything.

He is not faking his tears at the grave of Lazarus. Nor is He extinguishing His pain with the comfort of his own omniscience. He doesn't compartmentalize like I do. He knows it all, He feels it all. He stays a few extra days so Lazarus will die. And then He wants to rip His guts out.

What kind of God is this?

It's irrefutable. He is painfully strategic. All is subsumed to the greater good. In the Lazarus story he knows his audience. There is a game afoot and He will play it out to the last. He is determined to pull on the string of circumstance until it unravels as many curtains of illusion as possible, no matter how much it hurts those He loves. No matter how much it hurts us.

No matter how much it hurts Him.

At the grave of Lazarus an indelible picture haunts me: a man with the power to overcome death, with the power to alleviate His own suffering — that same man is sobbing.

In all my prayers of interrogation, I have wanted more than intellectual coherence. I have wanted God to admit that He is wrong. That Sam's suffering is not necessary. And I've wanted Him dead to rights because I had thought that Sam was the one in pain, not Him.

But a God who chooses His own pain fundamentally changes the stakes, not just for Sam but for every suffering soul. He is not only telling Lori, Sam, the boys, and me that it's worth it. In coming close and breaking His own heart, He is saying that there is something greater than His own pain. That's how much it's worth to Him.

A willingly suffering God, a God who chooses to be with us in our pain, means that there's something holy in Sam's suffering. In all of ours.

And just two weeks after Lazarus is raised from the dead, a scream from the cross will rend the air with an unanswered question: "My God, my God, why have you forsaken me?"

On that day, He will identify with us in our most stricken state. He will feel our excruciating confusion to the uttermost.

AS WE APPROACH HOLY WEEK, Lori takes from a box a small carved Jesus carrying his cross.

His shape is simple, and from profile, unmistakable. He is not walking upright. Jesus is bent under the load. He is down on one knee, dragging the massive beam behind Him.

Lori sets Jesus in the midst of a wooden spiral candleholder. On nights after Ash Wednesday, she moves yesterday's candle one more spot and lights it. As she does, the boys move the little wooden Jesus forward, following the light. He carries his cross past the towering candles, past the huge open faces of my boys who look on, entranced.

Lori reads a few phrases of liturgy, her face like Moses. She patiently answers Cooper's questions. Finley's interjections. And Sam looks on, silent, his clipboard of obsessions stilled.

Gazing at the circle of candles, something in me stops turning. I see the boys surround this spiral of light and the dizzying ride we're on slows.

I watch, dumbfounded: how did this radiant woman come here, come to live with me? By what means has this light, this beauty, this art, this presence of God — how did she come into my life?

Through the wooden nautilus Jesus walks. Past the stations of the cross, little Jesus carries the whole world. Feels all its pain. And my boys watch, night by night, as He moves toward the center of the circle, His face set towards Jerusalem.

Good Friday comes around. A gentle woman lights a final candle and the boys blow it out. And in the darkness, a wonder deeper than words claims the hearts of my boys.

Not just Holy Week, but every week, every day, she cups a flame, she guards a little candle in each of their hearts from the cold wind of the world. A little flame that will remind them every day of their lives: you were made in the image of God to create, to build, to incarnate His life on this dark planet until the whole world becomes a flame.

Easter came and went a few days ago and yesterday Cooper said to Lori, "I can see God."

"God is with us, yes," she replied, "but you can see God?"

Bathed in sunshine, my golden one answered, "Jesus is the light."

SEVEN
A HUNDRED BEES BITING ME

Advent comes around and I find a couple of Hot Wheels parked near the Virgin Mary.

As touchstones of my childhood, Hot Wheels can do no wrong, especially when we slide together those slices of cheddar-colored track. We set up the launch area, wrenching the track to the kitchen window sill. We run longer lengths down into the courtyard. The boys carefully choose each contestant and let go: gravity catapults the car, scalding upside down through a loop, and leaping off a jump like Evel Knievel, fifteen feet away.

And, after a lifetime of racing, Hot Wheels go into a peaceful retirement escorting the mother of our Lord to Bethlehem.

The same spiral candle-holder that Lori sets up for Easter, she does for Advent as well. And instead of Jesus carrying his cross, a carved Mary is astride a wooden donkey.

Cooper walks up to the spiral and takes hold of one of the Hot Wheels that has been left there. He looks at Mary. And then pauses and asks himself aloud where Mary is going.

"Will Mary go here, or there..." his voice trails off, and then concludes, "Mary will find her way."

In these days of waiting, I keep hoping for some candlelight. Like Mary, I'm trying to find my way. Trying to tamp down on the dialect of scold. And as I try to live up to the example of my father, I'm trying to live him down.

Dad was not, shall we say, a teacher. When he'd try to help me with my math homework, it would always end with him raising his voice in frustration. Dad could fix anything, from cantankerous tractors to appliances. But my confusion over algebra was an equation he couldn't solve.

So, the master mechanic and carpenter kept his skills to himself. And my role was relegated to that of a human lamp, my elbows and forearms a handy, moveable utility light for the task at hand. I always groaned when I heard him say, "John, I need you to come here and hold the light." But Dad never bothered to illuminate what was going on.

Even fetching a tool could bring his wrath. He would send me to the basement to retrieve a wrench and I would descend the stairs in dread, knowing I wouldn't be able to find it on his junkyard of a workbench. The sump pump clicked in the corner like a time bomb as I'd frantically search and then Dad would go off, yelling for a status from the top of the stairs.

So in hopes of being the teacher my father wasn't — and of bonding with my son — I took it upon myself to fix our dryer with my seven-year-old at my side.

I'd like to say that the apple has not fallen far from the tree, but I think this one beaned me on the head. And unlike Isaac Newton, I have no business anywhere near physics, or more specifically, electricity.

For a few weeks our dryer had sounded like baseballs were

careening around inside. In most cases this would've meant that my children had taken those Hot Wheels into the dryer as a final step of a make-believe car wash, but this was something else.

After I call Finley over, I realize why my father had not included me in his many fix-it jobs around the house: because I show Finley how to shut off the gas line. I pause in my instruction, but it's too late. I look at Finley. I make wrathful sounds. I say to never touch this without Mommy or Daddy.

He listens in that way seven-year-olds do when you talk about saving for college.

I shrug and unscrew the gas line from the back of the dryer. I tilt the dryer back and then prop it up using one of the wooden stools the kids use to reach the bathroom sink — which is all you need to know about where this is going.

Finley and I pop off the front of the dryer, but as we peer into it we can't find where the noise is coming from. The insides are not complicated. There's a motor turning the barrel. There's a heating element. And there's the venting, which starts at the lint trap and exits out the back. We start to remove this off, too.

But the last screw is tucked into a corner behind some sheet metal and I can't get the socket on it. We put the dryer back on the floor, remove the back, and I stretch towards that last screw from behind the dryer.

As I reach, 120 volts circuit my body as my left arm touches a loose wire inside the dryer. I make a very loud, shocked noise.

"Dad, was it like a hundred bees biting you?" Finley asks, concerned. I assure him that it was indeed just like that. Then I pull the plug out of the socket.

We finally get the vent housing off and discover the source of the noise: the small plastic fan blade is loose on its axle. I have to order the part online. So Finley and I put the dryer back together without finishing. I'm disappointed at my lack of completion. I tell Lori that I'm not sure what my attempt at home maintenance is teaching Finley.

Ever the sunny pragmatist, Lori says, "You're teaching him to unplug a dryer before you repair it."

EIGHT
THE VAST OPEN SPACE

I get up with ambitious plans for our Saturday. I announce to the boys that we will be holding our first "radio-controlled Olympics" and we set to work preparing.

I pull some scrap wood out of the garage and show Finley, age seven, and Cooper, age five, how to make a ramp by drilling the plywood into two-by-four blocks. Once they have the hang of it, I hand off the drill and go inside to check on the R/C helicopter and dune buggy. I pack batteries for Cooper's R/C boat and throw everything in the back of the Volvo. I'm excited; once we're at the reservoir, I'm going to have the boys compete for the farthest jump with the dune buggy, race the buggy against the helicopter, and let Cooper get his boat into some big water so he can really open it up.

An hour later we are stuck in traffic and hungry.

I look at the clock. Sam's keto diet has to be eaten at fairly strict intervals and I'm going to miss his next deadline. And the boys' excitement is now wrung out with impatience and boredom.

I pull up to the gate of the reservoir and curse under my breath

— cash only, fifteen dollars. I turn the car around, and Cooper and Finley immediately ask where we're going. I say that I've forgotten to bring money.

"Dad, how could you not have money?" Finley exclaims.

Of course! How can water not be wet and how can Dad not have money? Just the other day, Cooper asked me how much money I have. A few seconds into explaining our online savings account, he interrupted with: "No, Dad! Not money on the computer. How much REAL money do you have?" That's probably what's simmering through his mind right now: *Dad's computer funny-money! What good is it?*

All I want is a perfect day. To give them what I had. A bike ride in the golden light of sunset. Hanging onto my father's overcoat as our snowmobile chases a deer on a cold crisp night. Because those are the memories I lean on. When Sam's behavior gut-punches the hope clean out of me; when my clients don't call back; when it feels like Lori and I are living on some precipice of emotional breakdown; when all of these scenes are roaring through my mind and I don't know what to do — it is then that the indelible memories my father created become stones to stand on beneath the surface of this raging rapids.

The memories reassure and reframe. I look up. I see my wife reincarnating the same kind of moments. I see her, with an endurance I cannot explain, curate these sacraments of the true with heart-stopping beauty.

I see all their faces aflame around the Advent candles. Or foraging for carrots in her garden. I hear us laughing at Finley praying, "Father, son, and holy toast." And for a moment, all is right with our crazy world.

And today, I just want that moment to be my stupid little radio-controlled Olympics.

I drive away from the reservoir but like most Angelenos, once I'm off the freeway I may as well be in Mongolia. And as we plod through a no-man's-land of neighborhoods I've never heard of, everyone in the car grows more upset.

Everyone except Sam.

Even as Cooper and Finley's frustration with the day gets more vocal, Sam starts singing.

He's off-key. The melody is only vaguely there. But into my darkest blues comes the random rhythm of his clapping and the sound of my star boy singing:

"Holy, holy, holy! Holy, holy, holy!"

And although Sammy didn't sing the next verse, into my spent soul came the following:

> *Merciful and mighty*
> *God in three persons*
> *Blessed Trinity*

I get the kids fed at Chick-fil-A, get the keto into Sam, and then remember that we're near a different reservoir, Santa Fe Dam, a giant's bowl of boulders nearly a mile across, engineered to keep winter rainstorms from flooding the San Gabriel Valley.

We drive down into the dam and the walls of this circular fortress rise past the horizon. Immense rock walls tower a hundred feet from the gravel floor where we park.

As we get everything out of the back of the car, a stiff wind rises, spinning up dust devils. I try our little R/C helicopter, but the gusts blow the chopper like a leaf and I soon put it back in the Volvo.

We pull out the ramps the boys made and set up the jumps. I

make sure Sam has a turn, but he soon loses interest. He hands the controller back to Finley who immediately makes the dune buggy tear off at an insane rate of speed. Its front wheel hits the ramp and tips over in a cloud of dirt. Cooper cheers. The day has been redeemed.

I play with the boys for a while, then turn to look for Sam. He's gone. I peer into the distance and see him more than a hundred yards away, trudging towards the rock wall with his half limp of a gait.

He looks so small in that huge place.

I call after him and wave. He pauses. He turns around and looks at me for a second and then keeps walking, disappearing into the dust, a tiny figure in a vast open space.

NINE
BEYOND ABSURDITY

Faith hopes also in this life by virtue of the absurd, not by
virtue of human understanding. The paradox of Christian
truth is invariably due to the fact that it is truth as it
exists for God.

SOREN KIERKEGAARD

I love me some Kierkegaard: "...truth as it exists for God." Well,
there you go.

But I live on this sad soil, this finite realm where truth as I
believe it regularly collides with my experience.

Like today. I'm hiking with the boys to the north of Devil's
Canyon, off Angeles Crest in the San Gabriel Mountains. I try to
remember the names of the birds we're seeing as we make our
way up the trail. And far behind us, my own little bird is
moseying along.

We are on the hunt for Vetter Mountain Fire Tower. I'd picked this trail out of my old guidebook because I thought it would be an easy accomplishment for the boys; the fire tower used to be just a quarter of a mile off the road. But that was over twenty years ago and nothing looks familiar. The terrain has changed in my memory and I can't find the tower. And now I can't find Sam.

I leave Cooper and Finley and jog down, doubling back on the fire road.

There he is, bending to pick up a stick. I remember something the Floortime folks have shown me — using "affect." Throwing, if you will, emotional jumper cables onto Sam. Using a bit of drama to get him to understand when something is important to someone else.

"Sam, would you like to see the BIG, FIRE tower?" I say, exclaiming as best I can, raising my arms in a flourish.

"I would," Sam says, consenting to come along. As we hike uphill past the chaparral, I continue the affect. I make marching motions with my arms and legs and say what I always say when he's facing some stairs: "Big steps, big steps, big, big steps!" We stride to where the boys are waiting.

The low afternoon sun casts orange halos in their backlit hair. The wind blows through the fir trees, whispering a song with no melody. And as they each take one of their brother's hands, maybe Finley and Cooper begin to grasp a larger truth. In his clasp, perhaps they can feel what they can't yet express: that creation is not perfect, but in need of redemption.

THAT'S THE ABSURDITY. All around us beauty points to something straight, but life is bent. It's St. Paul's words in the letter to the early Christians living in Rome: *"...the whole creation groans...."* [7]

I accept that. But the absurdity is a diagnosis, not a cure. Some days I can laugh at how ridiculous it all is. But I can't laugh at Sam.

I have tried, I still try, to simply enjoy Sam as he is. As a boy who's well into grade school, but has the speech of a three-year-old. I try to meet him on that level and welcome the day for what it brings. For what Sam is now. And it works, for a while.

If only children could stay in their sloppy puppy state, with their mushed-up grammar and their verbal tenses all askew like their bedhead hair.

But they can't. We wouldn't want them to. One day, I want Sam to be able to interview for a job. Or to shop at a grocery store on his own. Yes, certain things we strive to build in our children — endurance, long-suffering, resolve — he has beyond his peers. He can be sweet and affectionate. Often has uncontrollable outbursts of giggling. And is delightfully unselfconscious. But I'm often haunted by the notion that Sam will be unable to engage, shrewdly and deeply, in the currency of life.

The day I left Illinois for California, Dad cried in our driveway, holding Mom. I'd only seen tears in his eyes once before, at someone's funeral. I drove off in their Dodge, rear axle creaking, the back bumper almost dragging from all my stuff. I was twenty-three, striking off on my own, taking an unknown plunge with no job and one person's phone number in my back pocket. I lasted till I hit the Interstate. And then, as the Talking Heads' song "This Must Be the Place" unspooled on my cassette deck, I started crying for everything I'd loved and was leaving.

I remember that free fall from the nest. How it felt to face that first plunge where I deeply wanted success. I remember buying our home and feeling like a kid with a new treehouse looking down on our little quarter acre and calling it my own.

I see these tests of manhood that lie ahead for my boys. While I will not teach them to extract their meaning from success, nor beat themselves up for failure, they are, nonetheless, rites of passage I want them to lay claim to. They are normal desires, from kissing the girl to king of the hill. And I want to teach them the right way to approach, to conquer — and most of all, to serve — in all these contexts that will inevitably confront them.

Finley and Cooper will one day drive away, do the same — but Sammy? Parents with severely handicapped children probably have a destination in mind. One day, they might hope for some limited independence. Maybe a group home. But what about Sam? Could he catch up to his peers? Increasingly, it feels like he will walk into adulthood with a developmental limp.

But then we keep hearing about the "plasticity" of the brain, its ability to recover, and we cling to hope. A thin hope that everything we observe is not predictive, not what it appears to be. A crazy, Old Testament kind of hope like a prophet declaring the impossible.

A hope that requires a willing disregard of the evidence.

As a parent, when do you stop longing for the miraculous, and start working towards the acceptable? When do you give up on old prayers and start trying to form new ones?

I was afraid all those years ago as I chased the sunset west. I was striking out on my own, plying my wit towards a new chapter. I had what every guy carries around inside him, the normal, will-I-cut-it fear. And eventually I found that when I put my head down and ran directly at what scared me, its power lessened every time.

And that is what I'll tell my boys. Whether it's their first gig at a club or their first day on the job, I'll say, *You've got this, you're the greatest.*

And I can keep saying that to Sam every day.

But will I ever get to feel what Dad felt when I drove away? A day when I'm blubbering like a fool but so happy because my baby bird is blowing the nest and catching a thermal?

When will this cycle of my hopes — and his counter-rotating spin of blank looks and cryptic responses — when will it end?

THE BOYS and I tramp up the trail for a while longer as it turns 'round the side of a hill. Still no sign of the fire tower. And then I groan. I see my car down the ridge. Like Pooh and Piglet we've gone in a circle. We need to get back for Sam's next diet treatment. I tell the boys we're done.

"But Dad, where's the fire tower?" Finley asks, disappointed. I tell him that we'll just have to find it some other day when we have more time.

We cut a new path steeply to the car where we happen upon an older couple who are about to set out. I ask them about the fire tower. They say that it was destroyed in a forest fire that roared through seven years ago.

Sometimes what you're searching for isn't there at all.

IT'S COLD THIS MORNING. Autumn has come. Gray mist garlands the cedars on Christmas Tree Lane.

I'm jogging, listening to a podcast where the preacher is unpacking a verse from The Revelation of St. John where Jesus calls Himself "the alpha and the omega" — in the Greek of the New Testament, *the beginning and the end.*[9]

The preacher poses a question: is there something else besides God that is your "omega" — some other endpoint toward which you're striving? Some other hope that takes priority over God?

Of course there is.

The foggy wind cuts through my sweatshirt. And silent questions from God go through my sternum like a switchblade:

> *What if Sam never grows up?*
> *Can he still know Me?*
> *If Sam never grows up, will I still be God?*

All my dread about Sam pounds through me. Tears wick from the corners of my eyes.

Jesus had a chilling story about the end of time when He will judge the world. He makes it plain how He will arbitrate: did you feed the hungry, give the thirsty a drink, invite the stranger in, visit the imprisoned? *"...Whatever you did for one of the least of these brothers and sisters of mine,"* He says, *"you did for me."* [10]

I know these things. I know that my good fortune, my home, all of it, is weightless on God's scales. Instead, He asks me to love those for whom the world has no use. Love the felon, the impoverished — everyone for whom the gears of the world do not turn. And when you do, He says, you love Him.

So, what am I asking my boys to become? And what am I worried that Sam will never be? Successful? Those rites of passage that I recited earlier — have I made them out to be an index of purpose? And if misfortune comes to my boys, will I have implied that they have failed?

I don't want to dismiss the vital gift that a passage of manhood provides in all of its challenges. But it is not the end, it is the beginning. It is the beginning of understanding that, well, what you thought was going to provide fulfillment, cannot.

Yes, those rites are there for a reason, but *passage* is the operative word: men *pass through* them to find that they can never be the goal. The woman you court is not for acquisition, but for you to serve. And the career you thought would bring joy can bring tedium; I remember how the boredom of my so-called dream job snuck up on me. Is this what I am pointing my sons toward?

No, it's worse than that: I have come to believe that Sam's deficits will make his own fulfillment impossible.

I open up the book of Isaiah, and revisit a passage I've leaned on in the worst of times.

> *Why do you say ... "My way is hidden from the Lord,*
> *And the justice due me escapes the notice of my God"?*
> *Do not call to mind the former things,*
> *Or ponder things of the past.*
>
> *Behold, I will do something new,*
> *Now it will spring forth;*
> *Will you not be aware of it?"* [11]

To me, Sam's future seems to be without category. But there is One who creates new things which have no category.

My world is so small. My future for Sam so hemmed in by the familiar. Why do I want to banish challenge? It is only through the imperfect and the broken that the miraculous is made possible.

Why do I insist on a boy's mind that I can understand, rather than being thrilled and surprised? Why can't I be open to being blown away by what I could never design or expect? What has happened to my hunger for wonder?

I want God to leave me be. I want a future I can comfortably predict, one that can be plausibly imagined. And in so doing, I am missing the little boy right in front of me and what he might become. I have wanted to put him in a frame, not let him paint the picture.

Oh, how I have wanted the titles and the tributes. To get picked at recess when I sucked at sports. For some girl in high school to see through the acne that painted my face red. To hear the hosannas of the corporate world.

Will I place my boys' feet on that same stepladder and lean it up against the same dead tree? Those branches cannot support their weight.

It's not Sam who needs to make a change, it's me. Me and my obsession with my bank account; my clinging to security; my fitful dreams for my sons all based in fear.

Sam's future is no less promised than anyone else's. That his destination feels opaque is not unique, but a reminder of my own false sense of control. It reminds me that it is God who not only creates each person's path, but imbues it with meaning. And it is God who will reveal it when its next chapter is ripe and ready.

I have not prayed for better dreams. I have small, tired ones. I need something that sees past the suffering. A vision that goes beyond the absurd.

I put down my Bible. I ask God a new question: "Can You make Sam great, not in the regard that I have lusted after, but great because he knows You?" And in the quiet I hear:

Yes, I can do that in anyone.

TODAY, Ally, one of Sam's play therapists, comes over. As she often does, she invites the boys to join her and Sam for a walk. Cooper tears off down the block on his bike with Finley in hot pursuit. Sam and Ally follow them down the sidewalk.

In Sam's right hand is Luke, Lori's old roller bag. He and Ally walk away following his brothers, chatting about whatever is going on inside that beautiful towhead of his. As he plods down the sidewalk dragging Luke, Sam wears his bike helmet, which he had insisted on putting on to match his brothers.

Off he goes, pulling his boon companion, carving his own unique trail. One laid down for him before the foundation of the earth.

TEN
HILLS OF DIM STARLIGHT

I wish I could tell you at this point that I stand corrected. That the words of old Isaiah are always at hand and readily jump to mind.

About now, it would seem right to say how each of our children must be held loosely. That each one has a future for which nothing is promised. I want to write some kind of dignified rejoinder, a mea culpa for all my doubts in the mayhem.

I have wanted to sagely say how I've changed because of Sam. That now, due to his jagged trajectory, I have lessened my so-called grip on the future. I've wanted to humblebrag, as the kids say: Am I not more *laissez-faire*? So much wiser for this, so much more free?

No, I am not.

Because the meantime is a mean time. Because amid the hopes that God would do a new thing, we endure the old thing.

Tonight, Sam goes off again, flying into a fit, digging in his nails and pinching as I carry him through the kitchen. All I want to do is spank his wrist, to go Pavlovian. I want to lead with my anger and let him feel a bit of what we are all going through.

But I don't. I set him on the counter and as he keeps hitting me, I keep hugging him, pressing my face into his belly and saying over and over, "Grace, grace, grace." I slide to my knees, keep my arms around him, and just repeat the word "grace."

The hitting slows, and the pinching stops, and then it is over.

So yes, I will pray for new dreams. For a vision beyond these broken moments. God could yet do the unprecedented, and make these episodes go away. If he can change me, he can change Sam.

Till then, I am baffled and worn away from worry. I am not a saint, I am a father of a little lost lamb that I have done my best to find but is still missing in these hills of dim starlight.

I believe; help my unbelief.

THE KETOGENIC DIET has been miraculous, but it hasn't pulled Sam over the finish line. In the first year on the diet when he was four, Sam's seizures dramatically dropped from up to thirty a day down to one or two. And from age five, to now at age ten, Sam's seizures have stayed at bay, the keto combining with two anticonvulsants to limit, if not eliminate, Sam's episodes.

But that last domino won't fall. Almost every morning, Sam gets in our bed around 6:00 a.m. and we wake to a sound somewhere between a whimper and a shriek, arms stiff, his face a mask.

We inquire with the UCLA team about cannabis oil or CBD. As it happens, a British pharmaceutical company is running a trial with UCLA, trying to bring CBD to the US market.

Right around Sam's tenth birthday, in conjunction with his current regimen, he begins taking syringes of CBD twice a day. At first, we see a 30 percent drop in his early morning episodes. But it's a head fake. While Sam's seizures became a bit less intense, the CBD contributes to bouts of diarrhea. We keep persisting, working with the doctors to get the dosage to a sweet spot.

But as spring turns to summer, his early morning seizures continue and for the first time in a few years, we shop for pull up diapers. We grind through one more smelly season, talking Sam through the embarrassment, and hoping something will improve during the remaining months on the trial.

ELEVEN
THE VOICE OF MY FATHER

In 2012, Cooper's first year, I landed a full-time job as a creative director at a local ad agency. But the account I had helped them win was eventually lost and I was laid off a couple years later.

The two years following the layoff started well. I reconnected with old clients, booked some work, and landed a large retainer. Lori and I had been able to build up our savings and I could breathe a bit easier.

But then the bottom dropped out again. I couldn't figure it out. I had done the same thing I had done for most of my career, dutifully sending out my latest TV commercial throughout my network. I'd even leveraged some serendipity; my beloved Chicago Cubs were in their historic World Series run and I'd written a spot for a Major League Baseball charity.

But the work didn't come. Was it the retracting advertising industry at large? Or perhaps now that I was fifty, was I yesterday's news? Regardless, as 2016 turned to '17 and then '18, the barometric pressure in our savings dropped.

I start a new video production company with a close friend

who'd shot most of my commercials. Eighteen months into our efforts we'd had a decent response from colleagues, sent out some estimates, had some good meetings — and booked nothing.

I lose sleep. Find myself losing patience with the one regular client I still have. Snap at the kids. And realize that I am wracked with shame.

A grand canyon opens at my feet once again. I can't measure up, to Dad, to my industry, or my mortgage. Anxiety seeps into every waking hour. I obsess about all the investments I could've made. I fret about losing the house and everything Lori and I have built.

I call Tim, my old therapist. While we don't see each other that often anymore, few people know me as well. He'd helped me get ahold of my issues. Talked me through days of desperation as I wondered, hitting my mid-thirties, if I'd ever get married. And he'd heard all about my father.

It's been a few years since I've seen him. I catch him up. Tell him about the book I'm writing about Sam and share the inspiration for the title. I tell him how my father would often say to me, "Remember, as you go through life, you're the greatest."

And then I dive into the dark well that has brought me to his office. I share how I can't dismiss my feelings of panic and anxiety, and worse, how guilty I feel about everything. Tim circles back to what my father said to me as a kid. And then hits me between the eyes:

"When did you link your greatness to your earning power?" he asks.

I stop cold. I can't answer. Then I get out: "Well, I guess those are the questions I pay you to ask."

I pause, absorbing the truth of what he's saying.

"I certainly didn't have any earning power as a kid, you're right," I acknowledge.

"And yet your dad said, 'You're the greatest' — do you believe it?"

I chew on my lip and can't reply. Fighting tears, I look away. I don't know what to say, but I know Tim has nailed me: No, I don't believe it. I can't accept what Dad always said about me.

Tim goes on, his soft voice full of compassion. "John, your father was saying that you are great by virtue of the fact that you exist."

"And that," Tim says, "was the voice of the spirit of God in your father."

TWELVE

I'LL FOLLOW YOU, AND YOU FOLLOW ME

I will even make a roadway in the wilderness,
Rivers in the desert.

THE BOOK OF ISAIAH

Just getting Sam from our minivan to the park shuttle is an adventure. His teenage cousins play sheepdog to Sam's wandering lamb. As I see my extended family having to corral him, I am dreading the hiking ahead of us in Zion National Park.

The day seems stacked against him. Sam doesn't do well in the heat and it's climbing well past 90. One of the rangers mentions that it might hit 100. Sam's cannabis oil regimen is causing him problems in the bathroom; in my backpack are wipes and a change of underwear. And inside me is a mix of emotions. Embarrassment for Sam and an ache at just wanting a family vacation, for once, to be postcard-normal.

Thirty-three years ago, Dad took us here on our way to the Grand Canyon. I remember looking up at the monoliths of stone and marveling at their grandeur. It had just rained, cooling the air. The sun came out, and the rock faces shone with a wet gleam.

But there will be no rain today. As the tram winds its way past the majesty of the Patriarchs, Sam melts into Lori's lap, his face reddened with dehydration. I stand under the pop-up sunroof and feel the hot breeze coming in. I ask Sam to drink and he sips sparingly from his water bottle. He's irritated, not understanding why he already feels exhausted.

His younger cousins, Abby and Ahna, sit near him on the shuttle, brandishing their new hiking poles. Lori and the boys, and my sister, Sarah, and her family, are to split off from Sam and me for the rest of the day. It wouldn't be fair to make everyone hang back as he lags behind. But I don't want Sam to miss this remarkable trail.

The shuttle reaches the end of the line at The Temple of Sinawava, the mountain that marks the trailhead. This was where Dad had turned around. He was never one for hiking. He liked driving, getting out at the scenic overlooks, and then driving to the next one.

Sam gets off the bus, and the crowds and heat do him in. He won't move. Doesn't want to try going to the bathroom. And then his nineteen-year-old cousin, Owen, hoists Sam onto his six-foot-five shoulders and strides down Riverside Walk.

I follow gratefully, but know what's ahead: The Narrows, a trail that not only follows the Virgin River, but is the river itself. Just ahead, Riverside Walk will take a left turn and disappear into the water where hikers grip their poles, steady their shoes against slippery rock, and trudge against the current. Owen will set Sam down, take off with the others, and — I don't know what will happen then. But I'm resigned to my expectations: at best, Sam will plod for twenty minutes and want to turn around.

He and I will grab the next bus down the canyon, and escape to the air conditioned museum.

The Walk ends, the river begins. Owen sets Sam down on the bank, Finley and Cooper jump into the water, and then splash on ahead through the shallows with their cousins, aunt, and uncle. I say goodbye to Lori.

Sam looks up at the Navajo sandstone soaring vertically on either side of the water. The Narrows is appropriately named, a slit in a geologic layer cake where sheer cliffs crop the sky. Over the course of nine miles, the canyon walls close in until the river is only fifteen feet across.

He stands there for a moment, moving his hands in his characteristic, contemplative way, each fingertip splayed out and touching the other, tapping, tapping, over and over.

I crouch down in front of him. "We're going to make it, buddy. Because you're Sammy the Brave."

"I brave," Sam replies.

"And no matter how far we get, I'll be proud of you." I loop my wrist through the strap at the top of my hiking pole, and take Sam by the hand.

The water is just inches deep yet Sam puts one foot in front of the other as if he's walking a tightrope. I try to steer us between the underwater rocks where the riverbed is more flat.

Our first obstacle comes, a small waterfall where the river gushes between boulders and falls a couple of feet. I try to pick a path where he can find his footing but the foam obscures my view. I take Sam's hand tightly and then stumble forward as half my hiking pole disappears beneath the bubbles. Sam gets yanked but doesn't flinch, doesn't freak out. We make it to calmer water.

Sam pauses again, looking upriver at his cousins who are striding out of sight.

"Sam," I say, "let's see if we can catch them!"

Sam agrees and we take another step. And another and another. We crisscross the river, looking for small sandy banks on either side. The cool water is reviving him. The red in his cheeks has dissipated.

But then the river bends sharply, and the water pools deeply in the turn. There's no bank. No shallow water. To keep going, Sam will have to wade in, chest deep.

We're halfway through when I realize that I haven't been using the pole to balance. It's been in my left hand, held above the water. And Sam's hand has been in my right; I've been leaning on Sam to walk. We get through the pool and look for another crossing.

Shallow and deep, slippery and sure, the process repeats, always different, always the same. Over and over, there's no clear way to cross, but Sam keeps going.

We get to a point where the current looks far too fast for Sam. I tell him that I'm not sure how to cross, but I'm going to do my best. Sam looks up at me and says slowly, "I'll follow you, and you follow me."

I look at him for a moment, his words echoing off the walls of my mind.

"That's right, Sam. You follow me, and I'll follow you."

I stare downward, hunting for spots where his sandals won't get stuck. I can't see a path. I hunt for larger rocks that afford a flatter surface. I'll need us to keep moving forward to keep our balance. We set out, Sam takes a step — and then falls face first into the water.

My heart sinks as fast as Sam. *This will be where we turn around,* I think. *Well, we made it a half hour anyway.*

He's wet and startled. I reach for his hand. He gets up.

Sam stands and looks ahead. Around the next bend in the river, we can see sunlight against the towering walls of the gorge: the countless tons, the weight of innumerable years pressing down forever, an alchemy that's turned sand into crimson gold.

But right now, those million years are as nothing. I just want Sam to not give up. For this moment to be a triumph.

There is no explaining what unfolded next. Sam takes my hand, keeps falling and rising, but most of all going, further up and further in with unspeakable, sure belief.

For another mile up the canyon, I watch in awe as my son claims greatness. Beyond my expectations. Beyond explanation.

And when his cousins and brothers see him, coming back down-river from where they've turned around, the shock on their faces fills Sam with pride. He beams. He's done it and he knows it.

And around one more bend in the river, perching on a rock and taking a photo of something beautiful, is my wife. She hasn't yet seen Sam.

Then she turns. Sees her son. Her mouth drops open in surprise and delight. And beneath that trucker cap, her eyes shine, brilliant.

Sam pokes himself in his shoulder over and over and says, "I did it. I did. I did."

GEOLOGISTS WILL TELL you this area of Utah was once a great sea. The layers of rock — the Moenkopi, the Kayenta, the Chinle — were laid down over vast stretches of time. Time so long that continents moved, the seas became a desert, and the water filtered through, gluing quartz to hematite and creating these stone sunsets of brown, ochre, and blood red.

But time stopped on that hot June day in the tenth year of my son's life. There, in some cumulative moment of creation, the weight of our years dropped away, washed by mercy.

In the grace of time, something cut through the stone of our terminal condition and said that the story was not yet over.

PART FIVE
THE BABY CROW

A boy's story is the best that is ever told.

CHARLES DICKENS

ONE

A NEW WAY OF LOVING

I hold the worn, sepia-toned photograph that has survived and shake my head in disbelief. The picture is undeniable proof that one of my father's taller tales did indeed occur.

It is clearly a summer's day on the Northside of Chicago and it must have been a hot one; Dad, fifteen years old, sits on the grass, stripped to his dungarees. He is leaning over a small animal, all his concentration focused on a small spoon he has pointed downward. Hunched on the grass, a hatchling crow has opened its beak around the edge of the spoon, and is looking at this boy — the only mama bird he now has.

It's 1943. The hardship of the 1930s has given way to the rationing of World War II. Food is not quite as scarce as it once had been. Still, you'd think every scrap from the dinner table would be too precious to waste on an animal.

But my grandfather must have seen the compassion in his son's eyes when he told him about a little crow who had fallen from its nest.

THE LAST TIME my father and I went somewhere together was his last Thanksgiving. Two weeks before that fateful trip to the timeshare, he and I went to look at some classic cars. As we drove north from his house, the wind picked up across the barren cornfields, blowing wisps of snow that snaked back and forth across the highway. I remember looking at the clock and wondering if the long round trip would be worth it; we'd only be able to squeeze in an hour of looking around the Volo Auto Museum before they closed.

But as we came in, stamping the snow off our feet, the guys at Volo welcomed Dad in and nearly let us have a run of the place, offering different cars for him to sit in and explore.

We found a 1937 Plymouth coupe, the same year and model Dad's father had owned. As Dad pulled on the door latch and sat down on the mohair seat, he was lost in reverie. Memories of his own father out of work, years before Pa could afford a car like this. Of times so desperate that Pa took his gun to a farm one night, shot a pig, dragged it into the back of his car, and roared off before the farmer knew what was going on.

On that wintry afternoon with me, Dad was still recovering from his quintuple bypass surgery. But as he walked from car to car, a bit of that sparkle returned to his eyes and drawn face. He pointed to various ones with his cane, and just like he used to do when I was a kid, he reeled off years and models by heart. We found a "Tin Lizzy" Model T. We came upon Model A Ford, and Dad talked about its flathead V-8 engine. We found a '46 Ford convertible, a fraternal twin to the Mercury that he and Mom had dated in. And as we walked into the final room, we saw it: a 1960 Bel Air, the first convertible he'd bought for Mom.

I sat down on the red and white houndstooth-patterned vinyl, and like so many times before, wished he would've kept it. He was just thirty-two then, but already living in a house he'd built with his own hands. He had a toddler girl and my older brother on the way. A young beautiful wife. And a career ascending just like the jet appliqué on the side of that Bel Air. We took pictures of each other behind the wheel and headed home.

In the dark along Route 59, we talked and I ventured a question that I'd been wondering about for several years, ever since Mom's dementia had begun to manifest itself.

"Dad," I asked, "how has it been with Mom? How are you handling it? I mean, Mom was your companion for fifty years, and now the conversations must be so different... how do you do it?"

Dad reflected for a moment and then said, "You learn a new way of loving."

TWO
BABY BIRDS

Like my father, Finley keeps finding little birds around our house. There was a sparrow who'd knocked himself silly flying into our bay window. And then, one morning, a baby California jay tumbled out of its nest and was limping about the backyard, trembling and frowning, its molty cobalt feathers still new.

Gentleness stole over my nine-year-old boy as he crouched near the bewildered bird, leaning over him with comforting words. He scooped him up, and those big hands softly enclosed the frightened, downy chick.

And one Sunday morning, Finley found a broken little bird in the kitchen. Sam was staring at letters, little plastic ones that magnetize to the fridge. The tray in front of him on the kitchen table held dozens. He stared, trying to arrange them so they'd spell out one of his favorite words, "motorhome." Sam has boundless affection for his grandfather's huge RV.

But Sam was stuck. He looked at the brightly colored lines and circles, befuddled. He was halfway there, having already placed "m - o - t - o - r" in front of him, but couldn't get it done.

Finley sidled up next to him, put a meaty arm around Sam's skinny shoulders and said, "Look for the 'H,' Sammy. You can do it, I know you can."

As Finley nestled in next to Sam on the chair and talked him through it, I just stared. I didn't want to move or utter a word. Plain and simple goodness was happening before me, unbidden, raw, and pure.

Lori and I have been careful about asking too much of the boys. We know how much they already sacrifice. But like it was something he did every day, Finley patiently talked Sam through the entire word until he had it and said, "See, you did it, Sammy."

I was shaken. My mind was a mess all morning, trying to reconcile what I'd just seen and what I'd felt for years. I had been so angry for such a long time, so bitter at the injustice, so unsparing in my accounting towards God.

But there was no denying what I had just witnessed. The scene needed no caption, but words came to my mind, one more time:

> *You thought you knew what goodness looked like. I am going to show you what goodness truly looks like in the abounding, unrequited love of your son for his brother. You thought goodness had been denied you. But you had no idea.*

I had thought it had been banished, but there it was. Goodness had come to my home. Despite my raging at God, despite all my doubts about any good ever coming from all the insanity we'd endured, goodness had come.

———

IT HAD BEEN a hard day for Lori, which is pretty much redundant in the saying: with Sam they're almost all hard. My wife's hands and forearms are scabbed and pockmarked from where Sammy left scratches earlier this year. Lori's neck and shoulders ache from all the times he yanks on her head for attention.

On this night, Sam was slow-walking his food and that's a problem. Because every drop and crumb must be eaten by Sam in forty-five minutes or less. And Sam was dragging that clock hand down to its final minute.

What happened next wasn't requested. But at the most weary time of a long day, Sam's youngest brother chose to lift our burden.

Without announcement, Cooper, now seven years old, got up from his chair and went around to Sammy's side of the table. He picked up his spoon, got some food on it and said, "Here we go, Sammy, watch the P-51 Mustang, it's coming in for a landing!" Cooper moved the spoon to and fro and then popped it in Sam's mouth. And Sam chewed, distracted by this new dramatization.

Cooper proceeded to get Sam done with his meal and then walked out of the kitchen to what I believe was the far-off sound of angels.

My baby boy, stepping into the breach and feeding our little bird with a spoon. And doing so with an aviator's panache.

Surely goodness and mercy shall follow me, all the days of my life.

THREE
MYSTERY AND HOPE

I still say it to the boys all the time: *Remember, as you go through life, you're the greatest.* So much so that they feel bashful and tell me to stop. But I can't help it, just like Dad.

When I practice pitching with Finley and he sends scorching fastballs to my glove that sting my hand? When I see him gracefully glide around a midfielder in his soccer game and then send the ball soaring down the field? He is the greatest, not because he scores but because the very movement of this boy gives me delight.

Lately, Cooper has taken to putting on some hand-me-down *Star Wars* pajama bottoms, which are still five sizes too big. So he pulls them all the way up until the drawstring is around his neck, his elbows moving inside them like billows, and then bounces, dancing, sliding and eventually falling in a fit of giggles, oh-so-conscious of how he appears.

And when Sammy starts his earnest prayers by saying "Dee'Zus" which reduces "Dear Jesus" to a one-syllable contraction? When he nails me with his preternatural insights like, "You be brave, Dad"? There are no words.

All of it keeps coming down around me, like fireflies on a July night. I can't contain what I feel for these boys, their foot bottoms black with sap and fingerprints clogged with dirt. It's all the greatest thing I've ever come to know.

Yet the joy doesn't leave me with answers today. It leaves me with a boy who needs his brothers. It leaves me with uncertain futures and wondering how it's all going to go.

Mystery does that. It inverts the commonplace. Provokes the need for the miraculous. It gets us shaking our heads and rubbing our eyes. Mystery says that everything is up for grabs and that the mountain just might move and be cast into the sea.

But not without purpose and not with some cynical shrug. No, this mystery is founded upon the Word that made the worlds. The One who insists that justice is coming. The One who says that one day, not yet today, but soon, the lion will lie down with the lamb.

This promised justice is the reason that the pain of life shatters like a blow to the face. We know that things are not as they should be. But in the promise of a great God, there is a time when it will be made right. Mystery is the testimony of the meantime. A brash declaration that what is bent will be made straight because something straight and true really does exist in the universe.

And more than just exists: that True One came close and felt the depths of my darkest nightmare. He came into my sodden finite despair that believed, when it was all up to me, I'd failed. And into my desperation that knew that nothing I could do could ever make myself or Sam or anything else right ... into that dark came a lavish, redefined love, a curation of heart-stopping wonder, and this mysterious, unbreakable hope.

It was God Himself in the person of His son saying, "Remember, as you go through life, you're the greatest."

WE'RE six months into the CBD trial and have only seen a mild improvement. And when I think about how upset Sam gets when he doesn't make it to the bathroom, it's been far more trouble than it's worth.

We go to UCLA to confer with the team. Sam's specialist for the trial, Dr. S., mentions an anticonvulsant that has been pairing well with the CBD oil — would we open to trying it?

Another drug. Won't it just be one more footnote on Sam's chart? One more data point on that downslope? I bring up the fact that most of the time, most of them don't work. He admits the numbers aren't rosy.

"I know," he says, "it's only got a 5 percent chance — but it's still a number. It's still five. Sam could be the one it works for."

We roll the dice, start taking the new drug — and Sam loses some of his speech.

And he had just started to read for the first time in his life.

His brave little words — "pat, sat, cat" — disappear in the drug's new power. But in the second month of taking it, the frequency of his daily seizures are cut in half. They just don't happen at all, for half the days that month. In the third month, October, there's none. No seizures at all.

We're into a successful November, but I'm pissed about Sam's words being slurred, and him regressing. We'd just heard him read aloud, for the very first time! I pull Lori aside one night and say that I'm done with the new drug. I want Sam to talk more clearly. I want him to read again.

"You don't understand," she says. "This whole semester, this whole fall, he's been happy. He doesn't pinch me anymore, doesn't scratch. And yes, I know, it's hard to hear him talk now, the way it sounds. But I can't tell you how much my life has changed."

And importantly, she says, there's more going on than meets the eye. His resource teacher and his reading tutor are both overjoyed; they can tell, even though he can't say much, that he's tracking. He's writing words. He is reading, just not aloud.

As usual, I'd missed it. We talk to the doctors and say it's amazing — no seizures for two straight months — but the speech thing... we're not sure.

Dr. S. and Sam's other neurologist, Dr. R., look at the chart. The CBD oil paired with this new drug — they're working. Could we try it a little while longer?

We do. It keeps working. Two months become three. And as Sam's eleventh birthday comes around, he puts four straight months in the books without a whisper or hint of a seizure. And then five months.

That's never happened.

All these years, I'd accepted the baseline. I'd looked at how much he'd progressed on the keto diet — thirty daily seizures down to one or two — and been so blown away that I'd grown satisfied. But what if Sam had still been waking up agitated all this time? What if that one stubborn early morning seizure had made him foggy and anxious for the rest of the day?

I'll never know. But I know what I know now. The seizures are under control. He's happier. And just last week I heard him say, "Pat bats ball. That's Pat's cat." That, and another ten sentences came haltingly out of Sam as he read to his brothers last night.

I came home tonight and Sam didn't run away. Instead, he smiled and pointed to his cheek to let me know where to kiss him. Then I pointed at mine and got one back.

Don't you understand? He will be great.

THE BOYS ARE GETTING out pillows and beanbags for movie night. I'm searching the TV menu for something on Netflix that won't have Finley complaining about nightmares. Last month, a very poor remake of Huck Finn had him in my bed for a week.

Cooper comes in and makes himself Finley's proxy. As I click through the thumbnails, Cooper says, "Now, Dad, does that movie have real skin?"

"Real skin?" I ask.

"You know," says Finley who's walked in, "do the people have real skin in the movie?"

Cooper explains that live-action movies have "real skin," whereas cartoons do not.

Sam walks into the living room carrying a huge bundle of blankets. That he'd managed to retrieve them out of the hallway closet was itself impressive. But he's never uttered what comes out of his mouth next:

"Would anyone like a blanket?" he asks.

Come again? Sam has never asked if he could do something for someone else, let alone stepped outside himself to actually do it.

His brothers' goodness, their compassion, it's spilling over the sides of his mind and changing him.

As I get the boys tucked in that night, Sam is laying on his bed, a big grin on his face, his fingers splayed out in his characteristic way, fingertip on fingertip, tapping them together. He asks a question aloud.

"What is life?" Sam says. "What is life? What is life?"

I lean over him, smiling and ask, "I don't know, Sam, you tell me: what is life, anyway?"

Sam says, "Life is, life is ... the greatest."

FOUR
THE BOY PIRATE

As the baby crow grew that year, he showed no inclination of leaving Dad. The crow took to sitting on Dad's shoulder and that became his perch all that summer of 1943. Having seen my grown father do that proud strut in his new faux-leather shoes, I can only imagine how he paraded around with a crow sitting on his shoulder. He was, I'm sure, a bit insufferable. The boy pirate of Skokie, Illinois.

One day, Dad got on his bike with the crow perched on his shoulder and rolled down Kilbourn Avenue. The fledgling spread his wings, and Dad felt the tiny bony grip on his shoulder loosen and lift. Dad's heart sank — was this goodbye?

Dad brought his bike to a stop and the crow fluttered back down to his shoulder. The young bird had made his choice; for now, he'd stick with the boy who'd brung him, and kept him alive.

And so it was that they spent that summer, the boy on his bike, and the crow he'd rescued flying above him, following him everywhere. Dad must have felt like a falconer out of some old tale.

I can see him now, rolling up to the soda fountain on his bike, chatting with his friends and, casual as can be, letting the flabbergasted surprise come over their faces as his crow hovers in for a perfect landing on his shoulder.

And here I end my story where it began for me: nestled next to my father and hearing his tales. Because this one, like mine, ends in a mystery. For I can't remember Dad ever telling me what happened to that crow.

Did he grow up? One day that autumn, did he get tired of waiting for Dad to come home from school and take off, never to return? There are no other photographs, no shots of an older crow living in Dad's teenage bedroom on some perch. Like Dad, the end of the story is gone, shrouded in the mists of time.

All I know is that a baby bird fell into his yard one summer's day. He rescued him. And Dad loved him in a way that marked him forever.

SHARE OUR STORY

Would you write a brief review? I don't have a PR firm nor a New York publisher. But I do have you, a growing democracy of readers who love a great story that stays with you.

Simply scan the QR code below with your phone to be taken to Amazon and share a few sentences about what you thought of *Remember, You're the Greatest*. Thank you so much.

GET MY NEW SHORT STORY AND A SNEAK PEEK FROM THE SEQUEL WHEN YOU JOIN THE BULLDOG & DRAM BOOK CLUB

I'm so grateful to you for reading our story. May I keep you updated through **The Bulldog & Dram Bookclub**? Simply scan the following QR code to be taken to our sign up page.

When you join, you'll receive the following ebooks for free:

A sneak peek chapter from my next book, "Keep the Faith," the sequel about Sam and his brothers.

A short story, "The Way Back," about my father's automobiles and my search for the perfect family car.

"Toys, The Director's Cut" - An exclusive to my book club members, "Toys," is a chapter that, while used in the book, got largely edited out of the final manuscript.

To receive all these stories for free, join The Bulldog & Dram Bookclub. Simply scan the QR code on the previous page with your phone and you'll be taken to my website's sign up page, or visit johnnybollow.com/JoinTheClub.

Thank you so much.

ACKNOWLEDGEMENTS

This book would not have come to be without my remarkable editor, Rob Wilkins. When I was twenty-two with barely a clipping to my name, Rob took a flier on me and let me intern at his magazine in Chicago. I'd never been a reporter. I hadn't even taken a mass comm class. But Rob saw something in my raw ramblings. Half a lifetime later, he poured through my inchoate pile of paper and helped me make sense of it. He told me to stick to the story. And saw a vein of gold in my father's benediction that became the title.

From Sam's earliest years, I would rip off a chapter and send it to my buddy, Greg White. After a few years of missives, Greg told me to "get out of the boat," as he likes to say. I committed to sending him a chapter a month till the first manuscript was done. Greg, thank you for your belief and exhortation, then and now.

Those chapters wouldn't have gotten written without my tireless in-laws, Russ and Kathy Chapman, who, on many a weekend day when Daddy needed to write, would take the boys on sleepovers. Lori and I wouldn't be alive without them. In giving us respite, they have given my three boys an amazing grandchild-hood of monster trucks, amusement parks, and literally thousands of arcade tokens. Russ and Kathy, I wish I could adequately express the gratitude that wells up in me when I think about how well you love us.

Over the years I have shared chapters with friends for their reaction and their pings back from deep space encouraged me to keep going. To those first believers, thank you: John Bird, Sr., Johnny Bird, Mark Chamberlain, Torry Courte, Johnathan Fisher, Lee Hildebrand, Glen Holmen, Paul House, Cairy Littlejohn, Marc Mealie, Kevin and Vicki O'Keefe, Santosh Oommen, Joel and Rebecca Russell, Izabela Szlufarska, Teresa Thomas, Basem Wasef, Annette White, and my amazing siblings, Bob Bollow, Sarah Woltjer, and Sherry McGowan. And to all the reviewers listed elsewhere who read an advance copy and provided such generous words of endorsement — I'm in your debt.

Matt Brennan provided vital feedback at the 11th hour — more than a few times. Christian Swanson provided wisdom, counsel, and calm as he has throughout my life. John Matthew Fox of BookFox was a native guide through virgin territory. Mark Dawson, James Blatch, and all the folks at Self Publishing Formula put a flashlight on the path. My dear cousins, Lee Bollow and Peggy Bollow Madda, reviewed pages about their dad. And my nephew, Jeremiah McGowan, a pilot who is carrying on the family tradition, advised me on some aviation aspects of Dad's story.

I am grateful to three writers who don't know I exist — Anthony Doerr, Mary Karr, and Stephen Pressfield. Doerr's exquisite novel, *All the Light We Cannot See*, was a structural inspiration. Karr's *The Art of Memoir* provided crucial guideposts. And Pressfield's *No One Wants to Read Your Sh*t* was a Derringer pistol of straight talk about story fundamentals.

A special thanks to my audiobook producer, Barrie Buckner, whose encouragement and coaching got me through the narration; and my longtime collaborator, Steve Goomas, who patiently recorded, engineered, and mixed magic in The Goom Room.

Konstantin Kostenko mind-read my ideas, sketched them to life, and then created the stunning cover art, all from 6,000 miles away in Poland. Cover layout, production, and endless iterations of kindness and advice was patiently provided by Lisa Young at Olive + Spark Design Studio. Vellum brought me the last mile. And Sarah Beach proofread the final manuscript.

To all those brave parents who toil in the fields of special needs — you're the greatest. As you go through endless rounds of advocacy; take on school districts when the IEP is wrong; don't accept the first or second opinion; and whose love for your child is higher than the sky and deeper than the sea, this book is for you. I hope our story is an encouragement to you. I'd like to hear yours as well. Please follow me @SpecialNeedsPop and say hello@johnnybollow.com.

Maybe my next book will be about my kind and cheerful mother, Shirley Timberg Bollow. It pained me that in writing a book about my father she didn't have more scenes. She once said that she wanted to give us "roots and wings." Indeed, her gentle humility was the curating love that made all our stories possible.

It's a pain in the backside to be married to a writer. I constantly have my face in my laptop trying to fix an unfixable sentence when I should be getting the kids ready for the day. Through it all, my wife, Lori O'Keefe Bollow, has supported this book without reservation, entrusting our tale to this imperfect stenographer. Baby, through all these long years you've never once had an unkind word while enduring my lopsided devotion to getting this book wrestled to the ground. You've believed in me and as Dad would say, you've kept the faith. I owe you everything.

Finally, to my baby birds who are beginning to mount up with wings as eagles — Samuel, Finley, and Cooper. Wait upon the Lord. Renew your strength. Run and do not grow weary, walk and never faint.

NOTES

1. "Time, O Time, turn back in your flight / Make me a boy again, just for tonight." Dad said this phrase so often that I assumed it was his own. Years after he passed, I discovered that Dad had been paraphrasing the first two lines of "Rock Me to Sleep," by Elizabeth Akers Allen: "Backward, turn backward, O Time, in your flight / Make me a child again just for tonight." As a boy, I thought all of Dad's aphorisms were original. But when I heard Steve Carell's character on *The Office* once say, "We're off like a herd of turtles," yet another illusion of authorship was shattered: we were chronically late wherever we went and Dad dealt with my Mom's constant tardiness with that same line. And that other go-to of his? "It's always darkest before the dawn"? That was English theologian Thomas Fuller, circa 1650.

2. Isaiah 55:12

3. Psalms 103:1-5

4. Isaiah 49:15-16

5. Genesis 1:9

6. Mike Scott of The Waterboys, "The Big Music"

7. Romans 8:22

8. John 11:5-6, 20-26, 32-35

9. Revelation 22:13

10. Matthew 25:40, NIV

11. Isaiah 40:27 and 43:18-19

ABOUT THE AUTHOR

It was the year of the fall of the Berlin Wall. Johnny, twenty-one, talked his way backstage to interview Boris Grebenshikov, the first Russian musician to get a contract with a Western label. Sitting on the floor of the green room with an open bottle, Grebenshikov looked over his purple-shaded Lennon glasses, poured Johnny a drink, and chastised all of America for the temperature of the wine: "Why do you people always chill it?" *Glasnost*, Gorbachev, and God — the Russian waxed eloquent about it all. The feature came out in the final winter of the Cold War and Johnny's writing career was born. An article about a Gulf War family was followed by more assignments from magazines and newspapers. But Johnny always came back to stories of real people, which landed him in *The Saturday Evening Post* with a feature on the forgotten women aviators of World War II, the "WASPs."

After transitioning into copywriting for ad agencies, the pull of the true-life story lay dormant until his 9-month-old son, Sam, was diagnosed with epilepsy in 2008. Confronted with a mystery that had no answers, Johnny began chronicling a ten-year journey that resulted in his new memoir of three generations of fatherhood, *Remember, You're the Greatest: How one special needs boy taught his father about love, God and everything else.*

Interlaced with his father's stories that recall the hardship of the Great Depression, World War II combat, and Johnny's own childhood in the Seventies, his book is eliciting comparisons to the non-fiction of Anne Lamott and Annie Dillard, and the humor of P.J. O'Rourke.

Longtime USC writing professor, Dr. Lee Cerling, summed up Johnny as, "One of those rare writers whose voice you simply want to listen to. You want to hear his stories, his anecdotes, his exquisite metaphors — you don't much care what he is writing about, because you feel that his writing about it will make it worth your while to pay attention; and that, quite possibly, if you pay attention well enough, you might learn something about how better to live your life in this mad, confusing, painful, yet wonderful world."

Born and raised in the Chicago area, Johnny makes his home in the foothills of Pasadena, California, with his wife, Lori, and sons Sam, Finley, and Cooper.

You can read about new releases, book-signings, events, podcasts, and music at his website johnnybollow.com. To invite Johnny to speak at your event or retreat, send a personal note to Johnny's company at the email john@bulldoganddram.com.

facebook.com/SpecialNeedsPop
twitter.com/SpecialNeedsPop
instagram.com/SpecialNeedsPop

Made in the USA
Las Vegas, NV
12 December 2020